D0287403

The Die Broke
Financial
Problem
Solver

The Die Broke Financial Problem Solver

Six Steps to Overcoming All Your Money Problems

Stephen M. Pollan and Mark Levine

HarperBusiness
An Imprint of HarperCollinsPublishers

THE DIE BROKE FINANCIAL PROBLEM SOLVER: SIX STEPS TO OVERCOMING ALL YOUR MONEY PROBLEMS. Copyright © 2000 by Stephen M. Pollan and Mark Levine. All rights reserved. Printed in the United States of America. No part of this book may be used or reproduced in any manner whatsoever without written permission except in the case of brief quotations embodied in critical articles and reviews. For information address HarperCollins Publishers Inc., 10 East 53rd Street, New York, NY 10022.

HarperCollins books may be purchased for educational, business, or sales promotional use. For information please write: Special Markets Department, HarperCollins Publishers Inc., 10 East 53rd Street, New York, NY 10022.

First paperback edition published 2001.

Designed by Elina D. Nudelman

The Library of Congress has catalogued the hardcover edition as follows:
Pollan, Stephen M.
    Turning no into yes : six steps to solving your financial problems (so you can stop worrying) / Stephen M. Pollan and Mark Levine.—1st ed.
        p.   cm.
    ISBN 0-06-661992-0
    1. Negotiation in business. 2. Problem solving. I. Levine, Mark 1958–   II. Title.
    HD58.6.P65   2000
    658.4'052—dc21   99-048468

ISBN 0-06-661991-2 (pbk.)

00 01 02 03 04 ❖/RRD 10 9 8 7 6 5 4 3 2 1

*The authors dedicate this book to Adrian Zackheim,
whose insight led us to the promised land
after fifteen years of wandering*

This book is designed to provide information on what the authors believe to be an effective way of handling and resolving conflict, as well as providing a guide to overcoming obstacles in negotiations in every realm of life. It is not designed to replace the advice of qualified legal, financial, or other professionals. Neither the publisher nor the authors assume liability of any kind for any kind of losses that may be sustained as a result of applying the methods suggested in this book, and any such liability is hereby expressly disclaimed.

Contents

Acknowledgments

The authors would like to thank: Gilbert Brim, Carol S. Dweck, Ellen J. Langer, John B. Morgan, Denis Waitley, Ewing T. Webb, and Reni L. Witt for their perceptive and intriguing writings; John Koten, editor of *Worth*, for his editorial courage and intellectual honesty; Erik Kolbell and Marilyn Puder-York for their insight and guidance; Stuart Krichevsky for his friendship and sage advice; Randy Newman and Jane Morrow for their extraordinary memories and continued support; the clients of Stephen M. Pollan PC for letting us be a part of their lives, and their lives be a part of our books; the late Gregor Roy for planting the seed; and Corky Pollan and Deirdre Martin Levine for saying yes.

Part 1

The Discipline of Problem Solving

There's Always a No

1

Tell him to live by yes and no—
yes to everything good, no to everything bad.

William James

Turn no into yes. Sounds too good to be true, doesn't it? I bet it reminds you of a pitch made by a former game show host during one of those Saturday morning infomercials. But believe me, this is no empty promise; it's real. You *can* turn a loan rejection into an acceptance, and a raise rebuff into an income increase. You *can* conquer your fear of starting your own business or shifting careers. You *can* solve every single one of your business or financial problems—and almost all your nonmoney problems too—using a simple checklist. And you *can* trust me. I'm not a former game show host; I'm a financial and legal consultant who spends his time helping people like you solve all their money problems and turn the nos in their lives into yes.

I believe a problem is anything that keeps you from being successful or that *could* keep you from being successful. I'm not looking to evaluate your problems or psyche any more than I judge my clients' problems or psyches. It doesn't matter to me whether they are real or imagined, or whether they are caused by you or someone else; they are still problems. I simply look at them as extant or expectant problems, equally worthy of treatment.

The checklist I'll be outlining in this book really does work with all business and financial problems. (It also works with most, though not all, personal problems.) That's because all those problems are fundamentally the same. Don't get me wrong: every single problem that every individual person has is, in some ways, unique. After all, every person and situation is unique; your career or business is different from everyone else's; your perceptions are different from everyone else's. But underlying the unique specifics of your business or financial problem is a sameness: there's always a no.

I believe every business and financial problem has, at its core, some form of no. It could be an outright rejection: "We won't loan you the money." It could be a stall: "I'd love to give you the raise but the company just doesn't have the money." It could be a rationalization: "You're more valuable to the company where you are right now." It could be a set of outrageous conditions tacked on to a maybe: "I'd be happy to loan you the start-up funds if you give me thirty percent interest and pay it back in two months." It could even be a self–generated roadblock: "I'm afraid to give up my job and start my own business." In effect, no is any roadblock or obstacle blocking you from getting what you want. Turning no into yes is the process of overcoming or hurdling life's roadblocks and obstacles.

Whatever kind of no you're facing, the very fact that it's there also means there's a possible yes: "You've qualified for the loan"; "We're giving you a ten percent raise"; "We're promoting you to district manager"; "I'll loan you the seed capital for three years at two points above prime"; or "I *can* succeed in business on my own!" In other words, I believe there's a solution (a yes) to every business or financial problem (the no). There's a way to overcome every one of life's hurdles.

NOS, OBVIOUS AND HIDDEN

Sometimes, the no inside a problem is conspicuous, as in the case of Mitchell and Beth Lewis.* They saw me as their last hope. Mitchell, thirty-two, had spent ten years managing a liquor store owned by his family. After the store had been sold, he stayed on at the suburban New York store, managing it for the new owners. Beth was a

*The names and some details of the stories of my clients have been changed in order to protect their privacy.

stay–at–home mom, who took care of their two children, Marcia, age six, and Nick, age three. Mitchell and Beth had been looking to buy a home for more than six months. They had finally found the house of their dreams, a Cape Cod that was close to Mitchell's store as well as being in one of the area's finer school districts. They and the sellers had agreed on a price and had signed a contract. But their hopes were dashed when they were rejected for a mortgage . . . twice. In desperation they came to me because they'd heard I could help people turn a no into a yes. Within two weeks we were able to do just that. We uncovered that Mitchell and Beth were rejected because they didn't show sufficient income on their tax returns for the size mortgage they were seeking. We, however, knew they could afford it. Mitchell and Beth turned a no—mortgage rejection—into a yes—mortgage acceptance—by explaining to the banker that they received a regular annual gift from Mitchell's mother of $10,000. Including that as income in their application allowed them to fit the bank's lending ratios.

The no was painfully obvious for Kenny Donovan, since it came directly from the mouth of his boss. Kenny, a forty-two-year-old managing editor of a well-known entertainment magazine, hadn't gotten a raise in three years. Like clockwork, every April he would go in to ask his boss, the magazine's publisher, for an increase. And also like clockwork, he'd come out of the office with a rejection. He came to see me on the advice of his brother-in-law, a client of mine who worked as an editor for a different magazine in the same company; him I'd helped land a raise. After doing some digging we discovered Kenny's publisher simply didn't value the kind of administrative work Kenny was doing, since he didn't see it as contributing to the bottom line. We developed a memo outlining how Kenny's efforts had, in fact, saved tens of thousands of dollars in the past two years. The memo also proposed new administrative efforts that could cut a significant amount of time from the production process, giving the magazine the chance to sell more ads and make even more money. By reframing his raise request in a manner his boss could readily understand, and refocusing it so it pushed his boss's "hot button," Kenny was able to turn a no—raise refusal—into a yes—ten percent salary increase.

Sometimes, however, the no isn't as apparent as it was with the Lewis family's mortgage rejection or with Kenny Donovan's failed raise request. Perhaps the no is hidden because it comes from inside another party. That's what happened when Grant Turcotte approached his uncle for a business loan.

Grant, twenty-eight, started an Internet consulting firm right after graduating from Cornell University's School of Engineering. Actually, he started it while still a student, by convincing his academic advisor to count his initial business efforts as an independent study project. Impressed with Grant's ideas, skill, and immediate success, two entrepreneurial engineering professors provided him with some start-up capital. That enabled Grant to seamlessly move his business from his college dorm room to an office off campus. But after two years in upstate New York, Grant realized he needed to move his operations down to New York City's "Silicon Alley." To do that, he'd need more money. The first person he turned to was his late father's brother Max, a retired IBMer who had always encouraged Grant's technology and business interests. Max Turcotte had more than enough money and knowledge to make the loan: since retirement he'd made a bundle on Internet stocks. Grant knew his business plan was sound, since it had already garnered him funds from other savvy individuals. Yet his normally empathetic Uncle Max turned to stone when approached for the money. That's when Grant came to me.

Rather than immediately trying to find other investors, Grant and I first worked on turning Uncle Max's no into a yes. Grant started asking other relatives about the situation. He learned that back in the early 1970s, Max had loaned money to bail another nephew, Cousin Edward, out of some personal trouble. Edward never paid back the loan and subsequently fell deeper into trouble. Since then, Max had sworn off lending money to relatives. Once we learned where Max's no really came from, we could work on turning it around. Grant and I developed a script for him to use with Max, to ask for a reconsideration based on new facts, and for permission to speak with his accountant. When an objective person, whose judgment wasn't clouded by family history, and who was also trusted by Max, supported the idea, Grant was able to turn the hidden no into a very clear yes.

Even harder to see right away are the nos hidden within ourselves. Jeanine Taylor came to me, saying her business was a failure, and looking for help in starting a new one. She described her wedding planning business to me. Jeanine was working three days a week, yet was making $75,000 a year . . . in profit. Her client base had expanded every year for the past five, and she projected further expansion for the next five. Her overhead was minuscule. She was up-to-date in collecting her receivables. Why, I asked, did she think the business was a failure? It wasn't exciting, Jeanine explained. After a few minutes of discussion it became clear that the no in this problem was inside Jeanine, not in her business. She simply wasn't getting the emotional gratification she wanted from her business. Jeanine loved the handful of media appearances she had made in conjunction with her wedding planning . . . in fact, she loved them more than the wedding planning. Together, Jeanine and I were able to turn her internal no into a yes by adding new services to her existing business. Today she's offering counseling on personal appearance and fitness for brides and their mothers. She's also now appearing regularly on a local news magazine, doing on-air makeovers for audience members.

THE IMPORTANCE OF THE NO

All this talk of yes and no is more than semantics. When you view all business and financial problems, whether they're obvious rejections or not, as nos, you set the stage for your being able to solve them.

Rather than focusing on all business obstacles this way, most people reflexively focus on their own situation's uniqueness and complexity. While I'm not a psychotherapist, I think that's probably so we can proclaim our "specialness," our individuality. "Sure," we think, "other people have been turned down for a raise. But my situation is different. No one else's rejection was ever so unjust or complicated as mine." Focusing on each of our business and financial problems as a singular, unique, discrete event may, in the short term, help assuage our egos. But, in the long term, it hurts us.

If you view problems as being unique, discrete, complex events, then solutions must be unique as well. That means we need to learn a whole new set of skills and acquire an entirely new fount of information to solve each and every problem. In effect, we need to start from square one with every single obstacle we face.

On the other hand, if you view obstacles as all being the same, as all being based around a no, you can apply the same approach to each and every one of them. If there is a sameness to problems, then there also has to be sameness to solutions. Remember, if there's a no, visible or lurking, behind every problem, there also must be a yes, apparent or yet to be discerned. Rather than starting from square one with each problem, we can learn from our past experiences, we can build on our victories. In this way, problem solving itself becomes a separate skill, or a discipline: the ability to turn no into yes.

In fact, I think problem solving, or turning no into yes, is the single most important discipline for any businessperson to master. Forget about becoming a financial expert, a marketing virtuoso, or a management guru. Become an expert problem solver instead and you'll instantly be master of all the other disciplines. You will be able to overcome all your business and financial obstacles. That will smooth your path to success. And nothing will do more to boost your confidence than repeated successes.

How can I be so sure of all this? Because it's exactly what I've been doing for the past twenty years.

THE EVOLUTION OF A PROBLEM SOLVER

Years ago, when I launched my personal consulting business, I had a hard time explaining exactly what it is I do. My kids used to come to me and ask what I did for a living. I resorted to my standard response to questions I didn't feel comfortable answering: "Ask your mother." Today, after more than two decades in private practice, I have a better answer. Now, when my grandchildren ask me what I do, I tell them, "I help people solve their problems."

Prior to launching my private practice twenty years ago, self-definitions came easy. When I was in my twenties and thirties I was a lawyer, practicing out of an office in Hicksville, a suburb of New York City. Next I became a venture capitalist, presiding over an American Stock Exchange–listed investment company called Royal Business Funds. After that I became a banker, working as the senior real estate consultant for National Westminster Bank. Then, I became a cancer patient.

Actually it turned out I didn't really have cancer, thank God. After receiving what I thought was a death sentence of advanced lung cancer, doctors eventually discovered I had tuberculosis instead. However, the miracle of my resurrection did not have a financial component. Luckily I had (and have) an incredible wife, four wonderful children, and a handful of good friends. My wife went back into the workforce to help supplement the disability insurance payments I was receiving. As my benefits and savings began to run out and our bills started to pile up, I started trying to figure out what I could do to make some money.

One of my closest friends, Gregor Roy, a college lecturer and struggling actor, was always stopping by to visit, trying to help boost my spirits. His good humor, thick Scottish burr, and joie de vivre always brought me out of the doldrums. But then one day, it was Gregor whose spirits were sagging. The telephone company had sent him a form letter threatening to cut off his service unless he paid an outstanding balance of $268. Gregor lived hand to mouth. Thanks to New York's rent control laws, he was able to get by on the small stipend he received for teaching a few classes and the occasional check he got for a part in a television commercial or an off-Broadway play. He simply didn't have the money to pay off the bill . . . and at that point, neither did I. But instead of us both wallowing in misery, a providential role reversal took place. It was my turn to raise Gregor's spirits.

I snatched the dunning letter from Gregor's hand, picked up the telephone, and called the collections department. Pretending to be Gregor,* I explained why the bill was so high and in arrears. (Gregor had been forced to make numerous international calls and then unexpectedly fly home to Glasgow for a family emergency.) I pointed out that it was a unique situation and that it was the first time the bill hadn't been paid on time. I stressed that I (Gregor) was determined to pay the obligation, but could only pay fifty dollars a month. I said that I (Gregor) desperately needed telephone service for business purposes. Finally, I asked the collections agent for her help. She agreed to the fifty-dollars-a-month payment plan.

When I hung up the telephone and told Gregor, he was amazed. He couldn't believe I was able to solve his problem so easily. I told him creditors want to be paid back; they don't want to write off the whole debt. I said people in debt actually have lots more leverage than they realize, and that often it was sufficient to demonstrate the willingness and ability to pay something, even if it wasn't the full amount. Gregor's normal enthusiasm returned. "Most people don't know about this," he blurted out. I realized right then that there was a market for my problem-solving advice.

---

*Since Gregor passed away a few years ago, Ma Bell has been broken up into Baby Bells, and the statute of limitations has run out, I've decided to finally confess our subterfuge.

With Gregor's help I developed an adult ed course (for an organization called The Learning Annex) on curing credit problems as a way to test the market. My wife had just begun working at *New York* magazine, and I suggested to her that I could write a short article that could help promote the course and my own services. A wonderful editor there, Debbie Harkins, helped me polish my article on getting a loan from a balky banker. My self-promoting efforts worked. Some of the people who took my course asked afterward if I could help them with their personal credit problems. A handful of readers of the magazine article contacted me at home and asked for help in preparing their own loan proposals. I was in the problem-solving business.

SOLVING ALL BOOMER MONEY PROBLEMS

At first, my practice focused on credit problems, since that was what I was teaching and writing about. However, I knew that I couldn't be a credit specialist and still pay my own mortgage. Credit was not only too small a market, but it also had inherent problems. With all due respect and compassion, let's face it: people with credit problems are not ideal clients or customers.

Much of my business when I was a young lawyer on Long Island, and then again when I was with National Westminster Bank, dealt with real estate transactions and investing. It seemed natural then that I add real estate problems to my practice. It was a serendipitous decision. It was the early 1980s and the real estate market in the metropolitan New York area was starting to boom, literally. Baby boomers, those seventy-six million kids for whom America built suburbs, swimming pools, and state universities, were coming of age.

I started soliciting real estate business at the same moment the leading edge of baby boomers were shopping for their first homes. Prices began soaring, since demand was far outstripping supply. Boomers who had been raised to expect that they would do as well as, or better than, their parents, were having a hard time affording the homes of their dreams. Knowing the lending business from the inside, and holding some unconventional views on home affordability and financing,* my approach meshed well with the needs of these young

---

*At the time, I advocated basing affordability on how much you could spend monthly, and borrowing the needed down payment funds from parents and grandparents.

people. And as the father of four baby boomers I also had a rapport with them and a respect for them that many other financial and legal advisors lacked. I was able to help my new clients solve their real estate and credit problems, and in the process, empower them.

In retrospect, it was this sense of empowerment I was giving them—the knowledge that they could turn no into yes—not the specific real estate advice, that was most valuable. That is what kept bringing these baby boomers back to my office for help with other matters. Some wanted advice on starting a business. Others asked for guidance on establishing a financial plan. A few wanted tips on asking for raises or hiring contractors to renovate their new homes. Today my practice involves all these matters and a few more. In the past few years I've been helping negotiate employment contracts and severance packages, setting up personal estates, mediating divorces, restructuring businesses, and reviewing business plans.

Sure, the clients who come to my office are unique in all the ways that New Yorkers are different from other Americans. They may spend more time selecting coffee beans than cars, more time dining out than grocery shopping, and more time at the gym than at home. However, in all the important ways they're just like all other successful baby boomers, like you. They own more and better stuff than their parents did at their age, even though they're earning less in real terms. They work in decision-making, policy-setting positions in large companies, or are running their own small companies. They read the *Wall Street Journal* and watch CNN. They have accountants and baby-sitters, mortgages and 401(k)s. They carry cell phones, laptops, and Teletubbies.

Rather than being based on one type of problem faced by all sorts of people, my practice has been based on all sorts of problems faced by one type of person: the middle- to upper-middle-class baby boomer. The matters I deal with, the problems I help solve, are all those that are impacting the lives of this particular demographic group.

Looking at my practice objectively, I think I've been able to successfully address so many different problems for a couple of reasons.

First, I had a very eclectic career prior to going into private practice. My background as an attorney, entrepreneur, venture capitalist, and banker probably exposed me to many more different businesses and situations than most people face in their work lives. Having such a diverse background made it easy for me to see the similarities among different industries and businesses.

And second, my cancer scare enabled me to put problems in a different perspective. When you're given a death sentence, other problems don't look so bad. Death is a real problem; everything else is just an obstacle. I thank God every day that my death sentence was commuted. Most people who survive a death scare develop a new perspective on what really matters. Some retain it. Others lose it as the brush with mortality recedes into the background and they go on with their lives. I've been able to maintain my perspective on problems, not because I'm such a deep thinker, but because I spend all my working hours dealing with them.

I've been able to help my clients with all their varied difficulties because, thanks to my background and experiences, I've learned to focus on the sameness rather than on the uniqueness of their problems. I've learned to find the no in every situation, and use it to guide me to the yes. That knowledge has helped me come up with an approach that can solve all your business and financial problems.

A Problem-Solving Approach

2

When you don't have any money, the problem is food. When you have money, it's sex. When you have both it's health, you worry about getting a rupture or something. If everything is simply jake then you're frightened of death.

J. P. Donleavy, The Ginger Man

Over the past twenty years, in the laboratory of my practice, I've distilled my approach to problem solving into a checklist of six items:

1. **Determine what is really your problem;**
2. **Make sure you're dealing with one problem at a time;**
3. **Focus on facts, not feelings;**
4. **Become an expert;**
5. **Create an environment of trust; and, if you need to,**
6. **Turn no into yes.**

Not every problem you face will require acting on every element in the checklist. Some, however, will. For instance, you may only need to use some of the first five items for expected problems, or perhaps just the sixth item for an extant problem. Unfortunately, you won't be able to determine which actions are necessary until you're actively involved in the process. That's why I suggest you literally view the items as a checklist, rather than as gospel. If you find one of the items unnecessary, simply check it off and move on to the next. I'll offer firsthand examples of using this checklist technique in the subsequent parts of the book.

1. What's your problem?

The first action on the checklist is to determine your real problem; in effect, to find the no. At first it may seem obvious. But often, the most easily perceived problem is either a symptom or a result of a different problem. Being unable to find a house you can afford might actually mean you're not earning enough money or that you're not ready for home ownership. Being turned down for a raise might indicate you're on the wrong career path.

Rabbi Jake Schorr came to my office at the urging of my youngest daughter, who had been a high school friend of his. Even though Jake's family wasn't particularly observant when he was growing up, he had always wanted to become a rabbi. After graduating from college with a degree in history, and then getting his master's in education, Jake earned his rabbinical degree, and was ordained as a Reform rabbi. His first congregation was in a small college town in upstate New York. His laid-back manner and focus on religious education fit in well with a congregation that consisted of lots of academics who were new parents. He also enjoyed working in a relaxed, open–minded, small town setting. But after three years his wife grew homesick for the metropolitan New York City area. He knew that in order to increase his income he'd need to move to a larger and more established congregation. He began looking for a new job. It didn't take long.

Jake quickly landed an interview with a large, affluent congregation in a suburban town just north of New York City. While it was a congregation whose members were older than what he was used to, the president stressed that they actually were looking for a child-centered rabbi: membership was shrinking, and the board wanted to encourage younger families to join. But Jake, though intelligent and articulate, isn't the most charismatic presence. In appearance and manner he is more like Billy Crystal than Tony Robbins. That didn't seem to matter to the board. After a month-long interview process he was hired and given a generous salary and a three-year contract.

During the middle of that third year he came to see me. The board's focus on education had lasted only eighteen months, just long enough to show a small increase in membership. After that point Jake began fielding complaints from the board about his sermons. He took the comments as constructive criticism, and worked hard at improving his speaking and sermonizing. As soon as those criticisms died down, other problems arose. The younger congregants, looking to play a more active role in the congregation, were working to unseat the old guard. Jake, whose sympathies lay with the young people but who was hired by the old guard, was caught in the middle. He had come to me for advice on how to navigate this minefield while negotiating a contract extension.

After speaking with Jake for about forty minutes I could see that there was far more to his problem than just negotiating a contract extension. I asked him why he had become a rabbi. He said it was to work with children whose love of God was fresh and pure. I asked him if that was what he was doing. Not as much as he'd like, he explained. I asked him how he would feel if we managed to get him a contract extension. Secure, he responded immediately. Not happy, I noted. Did he think that if we overcame this problem it would be relatively smooth sailing at this congregation. He laughed. After a few minutes of this conversation the scales started falling from Jake's eyes. He saw that his real problem wasn't negotiating a new contract and managing the congregation's politics; it was finding a new job. The no, or obstacle, in the situation was his job, not his contract.

With that as our focus, Jake and I worked on a plan. He asked for a one-year extension of his contract with no salary increase, saying that he thought it important the congregation devote its energies to working on its other problems rather than engaging in a potentially divisive negotiation with the rabbi. At the same time he began putting out discreet feelers about other congregations. After eight months of subtle investigations he found a smaller and younger synagogue, located in a more remote suburb, that seemed a better fit than his still contentious congregation. While the initial salary offer from the new congregation was for ten percent less than he was currently making, the proposed contract was for ten years with six percent annual increases. Jake signed.

That was seven years ago. I recently saw Jake again at a barbecue at my daughter's house. Things are going so well that the congregation wants to preemptively extend his contract until he reaches retirement age. I gave him my blessing.

2. One problem at a time

The second action on the checklist is to make sure you're focusing on a single problem—on just one no—rather than on a whole family of problems—or cluster of nos. Hating your career is certainly problematic, but it's a large general difficulty that encompasses a set of smaller more specific hurdles. You're not Superman. You can't go from the starting line to the finish tape in a single bound. Try to, and you'll end up failing and frustrated. Instead, you need to break the race down and work at overcoming each individual hurdle. You need to divide that one giant no into a set of smaller nos.

Frustrated is an understatement for how Vince Cerano felt when he first came to see me. From his outward appearance, however, Vince seemed totally together. Impeccably dressed and groomed, with a deep tan and the handsome good looks of a young James Caan, he seemed the personification of self-confidence. The veneer crumbled after two minutes in my office. Vince began recounting an endless stream of problems, and recounting them at such a rapid rate that even I, with years of experience listening to New Yorkers, couldn't keep up. After I finally got him to slow down I was able to piece together the story.

Vince was a home builder. For five years he had owned his own carpentry business. He was doing okay financially, but hungered for more. Vince had grown up in an upper-middle-class family. Both his parents were schoolteachers. Though they outwardly accepted his desire to work with his hands, he always sensed they were somewhat disappointed in his choice of professions. When two other contractors, a roofer and a foundation specialist, came to him with the idea of forming a partnership, he jumped at the chance.

For a few years things were great. The three partners began by buying odd lots in already developed areas and putting up individual, single-family homes. With all three of them working on each job they were able to keep costs under control and meet their deadlines. They'd take the profit from one job and use it to finance the next. Eventually they also moved into renovation work, gutting and renovating "handyman specials," and then reselling them for a tidy profit. Finally, after five years, they bought a large plot of land in an exurban area. One of Vince's partners had learned that a new corporate park was about to be built nearby, dramatically increasing the demand for homes. The three partners, subcontracting out much of the work, quickly built ten nouveau Victorian homes, sold them all, and made a small fortune.

From there the business boomed. It now made less and less sense for the partners to do any of the actual work themselves. In fact, the former foundation specialist bought a winter home in Florida and announced his intention of spending more time golfing than pouring cement. The now ex-roofer divorced his wife of twenty years, bought an Italian sports car he could barely squeeze into, and was spending a small fortune wining and dining, allegedly for the company. Vince's tastes ran more to Hugo Boss suits and weekly manicures. After only two years of this type of extravagance the bottom began to fall out of the business.

Because the three partners were so busy spending money, there wasn't sufficient supervision of one of the company's developments. Not only was it delayed and over budget, but the final workmanship was shoddy. The first handful of homeowners who had bought off the plans and the model complained bitterly about the problems as soon as they took up residence. Vince and his partners hadn't kept any financial cushion, and they had tapped their credit out building the development. In order to pay for the necessary repairs they needed to sell more of the homes. But the current homeowners made sure to warn every visitor about the situation. The homeowners then sued Vince's business. The construction loan fell into arrears and the bank was threatening to take over the development. And with the business in a nosedive Vince had no income. He could no longer afford the mortgage on his *own* house.

Vince came to me in search of a magic bullet: a quick, painless cure to all his business problems; basically he wanted my help in turning back the clock. It took me a good hour and a half to unravel all the threads in Vince's story. And in that time I tried to point out to him that he wasn't facing one problem—a failing business—he was facing a cluster of interconnected problems. I suggested that it was his attempt to solve all his problems at once that was leading to his frustration and feeling of impotence. Instead, I urged him to start examining each problem individually.

Together we compiled a prioritized list of his problems. Though he had been focusing on his business, it was clear that Vince's most important problem was his lack of a stream of income. Without money coming in the most pressing nos for Vincent were no food on his family's table and no roof over their heads. We made getting a job his first goal. Simply by concentrating on one specific obstacle, Vince's spirits stabilized. Within four weeks Vince found work as a construction manager for a firm he had worked for and with in the past. It wasn't the income he was used to, but it did keep the wolves from the door. Those first two nos had been turned to yes.

Over the course of the next two years I worked with Vince, dealing with one problem after another. At one point in the process he accepted that rather than trying to save his business he should just try to disentangle himself from the whole mess. Today, Vince is in business once again—as a partner in the construction management business he first joined as an employee.

3. Focus on facts, not feelings

The third item on the checklist is to insure that each of your individual hurdles is framed rationally, not emotionally. All rational problems can be solved by applying logic and facts. Many emotional problems can't be solved, only mitigated. And some emotional problems can't be solved at all. Thankfully, all business and financial problems can, in fact, be viewed rationally. Unfortunately, the same isn't true for all personal problems. That's why I tell people my approach can help them solve *all* their business problems but only *most* of their personal problems.

Gloria Summers is one client I *couldn't* get to frame her problem rationally rather than emotionally. Gloria had every right to be angry about her situation. A tall, willowy woman with closely coiffed auburn hair, Gloria was one of the dozen founders of New York's most profitable public relations agency. The agency was actually a consortium of twelve different small specialized boutiques that came together under one roof to lower overhead and simultaneously expand their reach. The idea worked. Gloria's shop wasn't one of the larger divisions, but it was quite profitable. She had annual revenues of over $2,000,000.00. For more than two decades the consortium was a great success. That's why it came as such a shock when Gloria was called into the president's office one Monday and told she was fired.

Gloria had always thought of herself as an owner, even though she was technically an employee. She simply couldn't believe what was happening. She was offered two years' severance pay and her full pension, but she was also asked to be out of the office by the end of the week. She came to my office the first thing the next day.

After speaking with her it was clear to me that Gloria's firing was questionable. Despite her youthful appearance, she was sixty-four years old. There had never been any previous mention of poor performance. In fact, after a three-year slide in her division's revenues they had just rebounded to their highest level in five years. Her profit margins had always been high. It certainly appeared she was being terminated because of her age. I told her we had an excellent chance to get a very large settlement based on her not only being wrongfully terminated but also because she was a founder and de facto part owner of the business. Gloria didn't seem to care about the money, however. Rather than the fear I usually see in recently terminated clients, Gloria displayed an eerie calmness. She said she wanted justice, nothing less.

I tried to explain to Gloria that justice was an emotional goal and she would be better off trying to get them to literally pay for what they'd done and then wipe her hands of the whole situation. She seemed to agree. I immediately drafted a letter to the president of the agency, telling him that I had been hired by Gloria and that we would be contacting him with a counteroffer.

My staff and some outside specialists started to do some research into both her case for wrongful termination and the finances of the agency. We believed we had a good case for age discrimination. In addition, while the finances were somewhat convoluted, it appeared that Gloria was a fifteen percent owner of the agency. We presented our arguments in writing to the agency and asked if they would now like to change their termination package. They did. The attorney for the agency came back with an astounding $3 million settlement offer. The outside specialists and I were ecstatic. The sum was more than we ever dreamed. Gloria, on the other hand, was unmoved.

She coolly said that if they were willing to offer $3 million that meant her ownership share had to be worth more. I tried to explain to her that, while she might be right, it would be difficult to prove in court. I added that if we went to trial it would cost a great deal of money and take a great deal of time. Gloria didn't care. She wanted justice, whatever the cost. I tried to change her mind, but she just grew more distant. I passed her case on to a litigation specialist. That was four years ago. The case still hasn't been settled. I don't know how Gloria is paying her bills in the meantime. I wish her well. Still, I'm afraid that in looking for "justice" rather than a settlement she'll never find satisfaction.

4. Become an expert

The more information and knowledge you have about your situation or other parties with whom you're dealing, the easier and quicker you'll solve your problem and turn a no into a yes. Nothing is too trivial. Sometimes, information comes from traditional sources; other times, it requires some ingenuity to ferret out. But often it takes more than knowledge for expertise to be effective. You may also need to demonstrate your authority. Expertise can usually be demonstrated subtly. Other times it might need to be shown more blatantly, such as through an academic credential.

At first glance, Kevin Halleck seemed already to be an expert in his company—after all, he was president of one of its divisions. Bookish and prim, his conservative banker's garb and maître d' manners matched his analytical, ever rational, and supremely polished approach to business and life. But Kevin was soon to learn that, sometimes, knowledge lies between the lines of a financial statement and emotions count more than numbers.

Kevin came to me after being frustrated two years in a row by his inability to get either a salary increase for himself or a budget increase for his division. Kevin ran the consumer magazine division of a publishing company. While most of the company's revenues came from its textbook publishing and trade magazine publishing arms, Kevin's division was far from a money loser. Because his publications had to stand out on the newsstand, Kevin's printing costs were higher than those of the other divisions. In addition, he had to spend more on staff and freelance writers and photographers. Still, Kevin made a small profit for the company every year. In addition, he knew that the board enjoyed the public exposure his magazines brought the company. Yet despite all that, Kevin hadn't been able to get any further funds for either himself, his staff, or his publications.

Kevin had made the case that in order to boost the long-term profitability of the magazines the company needed to invest a bit more in the short term. He had ferreted out all the numbers, researched the competition, and put together projections that backed up his argument. Yet for two years now Kevin had been unsuccessful. The board listened politely, said they'd consider his proposals, but then sent word that they'd decided to maintain the status quo; bluntly put, they said no. Kevin's staff was beginning to get frustrated. So was he, and that's why he came to see me.

Together we went over the situation closely. It was obvious that Kevin knew the numbers cold and that his argument seemed correct. There was something missing, some vital piece of information we lacked. I sent Kevin out to learn more about the individual board members, rather than the company's numbers.

First he did some online research and dug up biographies of all the board members. He learned where they went to school, what charities they favored, and where they lived. Kevin knew from company gossip that it was the chairman who ruled the roost, and so he concentrated his research efforts on him. Eventually, while digging in the stacks of a local business school library, he found an interesting magazine. It was an old issue of a publishing industry magazine that contained an interview with the chairman back when he had first put together the company. The company had been formed when the chairman had used venture capital to acquire three small unrelated publishing businesses. In the interview, the chairman, then president, explained his business strategy. He said that he thought publications or imprints could either be cash cows or award winners, but not both. A successful company, the chairman opined, should have a trophy division in order to present a pretty face to the world, but really needed to rely on cash cows which, while less glamorous, were the real moneymakers.

Kevin called me from a pay telephone in the library. He'd uncovered the real, previously hidden reason for the no: his part of the company was the trophy division. Later that afternoon when he stopped by my office we examined the situation. It was clear that no matter what Kevin did he wasn't going to get any greater share of the company's resources for either himself, his staff, or his publications. The company didn't really care about increasing his division's profitability. All that mattered to the board was that Kevin's magazines gave the company a pretty face. The answer was now clear. Rather than trying to come up with ways to get more money from the board, Kevin and I started trying to find him another job.

5. Create an environment of trust

Focus, clarity, and knowledge will together solve many problems. But another element is needed to guarantee success: trust. Unfortunately, in today's fast-paced business world there isn't enough time for trust to develop naturally. Instead, you need to expedite it by showing—through a host of measures including your language, action, garb, and timing—that you care about everyone else you need to help solve your problem.

John Stavros remains one of the most difficult clients with whom I've ever had to work. In his midseventies when I first met him, John was short and muscular. His deeply tanned, leathery face was set off by a full head of white hair. A flamboyant dresser, he prided himself on his brightly colored suits and matching ascots. He regaled everyone he met with the tale of how, alone, and with nothing more than the clothes on his back, he came to this country from Greece at the age of twelve. He began his business career by selling gyros from a pushcart across the street from St. Patrick's Cathedral in Manhattan, and through his hard work and genius—John actually used that word—built up an empire of diners and catering halls. John punctuated his tale with four letter words and repeated finger pokes in the chest. While his story *was* inspiring, it was unpleasant to hear him tell it . . . over and over.

John had come to me because he had heard I had a good track record of negotiating with banks. His relationship with his bank certainly needed some help. John's bank had made quite a bit of money with him over the years. They had financed his restaurant acquisitions and expansions, as well as his forays into catering. The problems began when he started a massive remodeling program on his catering facility. Buying this sprawling architectural monstrosity, located on a major commercial thoroughfare in an affluent suburb, wasn't enough for John. He had to remake it in his own image. *Garish* was the word I politely used to describe the result. *Financial quagmire* was the phrase the bankers used.

Since John had no patience for those who didn't share his taste or views, he hadn't even bothered to speak with the increasingly nervous bankers. Costs kept running higher, the schedule kept being pushed back, and John's representatives kept coming back to the bank for more. Like most bankers, John's were loath to write off a loan—particularly a large one—so they continued to lend him enough money to keep the debt on the books. They did try to exert some influence, however. But whenever they would telephone or come to John's office they were treated contemptuously. When told they were at the office, John would curse—loud enough for them to hear. When he did come out to see them he would say he was too busy to talk to them, and would suggest that one of his staff show them around. Even bankers have their limits. They sent John's accountant a letter announcing their intention of calling his lines of credit within six months. That's when his office called me.

After hearing the whole story from the accountant—John was, of course, too busy to see me—I insisted on a personal meeting with John. Figuring I had nothing to lose by being bold, I laid it on the line with John. His bankers simply didn't trust him anymore. He was treating them like minions, pushing them around, and not even bothering to hide his disdain for them. They weren't his minions, I pointed out. In fact, it was within their power to destroy John's entire operation, the string of pushcarts, the chain of diners, and yes, even his colossus catering hall. He needed to rebuild their trust in him. He had to show them that he respected them and even cared for them. And he needed to start right then. I held my breath and prepared for an onslaught. The curses did indeed come, but this time they were self-directed. Of course, after ripping himself to shreds he did finally turn to excoriating the bankers. But by then he'd run out of his better epithets. Luckily when he turned to me he was totally out of ammunition. All he did was ask what he should do.

Every week for the next six months, John and I attended meetings at the bank's headquarters. I had John dress in a conservative blue suit with white shirt and a red tie rather than an ascot. I worked with him for two hours before each meeting on exactly how to be deferential to the bankers. I have to say that John worked as hard at holding his tongue as he did in building his fortune. He prayed for ten minutes before every meeting in an effort to calm down. After the first four meetings, the bankers were still unmoved. They thought John's transformation was a sham. After the second month of meetings they were still unconvinced, but were willing to listen to our proposals. After the third month they were a bit more open to negotiating. Then in the middle of the fourth month the ice broke. They and John actually shared some unforced, unplanned pleasantries. At the end of five months the restructuring deal was on the table. And after six months a deal was signed.

6. Turn no into yes

Often, all your efforts up until this point will be enough to get a yes. But sometimes they won't be sufficient, and you'll still come face-to-face with a rejection. Most people, when faced with a rejection, back down. But to truly solve all your business problems and become successful, you need to master the sixth item on the checklist and learn how to turn rejections around, how to literally turn a no into a yes. That requires you to look behind the no, learn where it came from and why. Those are the keys for turning it around.

David Timmons was a friend of mine long before he became a client. As the human resources director for the New York office of a major international entertainment company, he had sat on the opposite side of the table from me in many employment contract negotiations. As often happens in business, our respect for each other as adversaries blossomed into friendship.

Divorced, but still a devoted father to his seventeen-year-old son, David lived an almost monastic life for an affluent New York bachelor. Balding, and with a runner's physique, he even looked monkish. Up at five, he was at his health club by six and his desk by eight. He didn't leave there most nights until twelve hours later. Weekends were devoted to his son, who came into town from Connecticut every Friday night and didn't leave until Sunday afternoon. His devotion to his company was second only to his son. He was a beloved figure in the organization, serving as father-confessor to most of the middle-level executives in the company. That's why when he called to tell me he'd just been terminated I was almost as shocked as he.

When he came to my office later than afternoon and described what had happened things got even more confusing. David had been called into an early morning meeting with the three executive vice presidents who, effectively, ran the company. David was on very good terms with two of the executives but did have some minor run-ins with the third. One executive recounted David's exemplary record and string of outstanding evaluations. The second described what a positive impact David had on employee morale throughout his tenure. And then the third terminated him, presenting David with a woefully inadequate severance package and no explanation.

The whole scenario sounded strange. While all termination meetings are scripted, this script seemed to be written by David Lynch. In almost every termination case I tell my clients to forget about trying to reverse the decision—why would you want to work for someone who fired you—and instead, to concentrate on getting the best possible severance package. I couldn't do that here, however. Not only did something smell fishy, but David also was so psychologically tied to his company that he couldn't just let go. I knew that emotionally he'd have to at least make an effort to reverse the decision. I told David that the key to doing that was to look behind the no.

From my outer office, David placed calls to the two executive vice presidents who spoke positively about him at the meeting. Both essentially told David the same story. The third executive vice president, whose responsibility was primarily financial, was under pressure from the board because of the increased payroll of the company. In an effort to deflect blame from himself, he said that the problem was David's inability to hold the line in contract negotiations, noting that David was more concerned with being well liked than running a tight ship. The other two executive vice presidents didn't feel they could directly contradict their peer. As a result, David got the ax. Both said that if they could do anything to help, they would.

Now realizing what had happened, David and I planned a counterattack. The next morning he presented a memo, not just to the three executive vice presidents, but to the entire board as well. David recounted the entire situation, stressing his flawless record, his years of loyalty, and the esteem in which he was held by the entire company. Rather than asking the company to reverse course and give him his old job back he accepted that decision but added new facts to the equation. David proposed that he be shifted into a newly created strategic recruitment post. The two executives who liked David immediately read between the lines of our memo. They saw that we were offering a way for everyone to "save face," and for David to stay with the company. They added covering memos to ours, supporting

David's idea. He was hired back into the company the very next day.

Within eight months the human resources director position in the company's West Coast office opened up. David lobbied for, and landed, the job. His son starts classes at UCLA next year.

FROM MONEY SUCCESS TO PERSONAL HAPPINESS

Turning No into Yes is more than just an approach for solving business problems and achieving career success. It's also a program for creating personal happiness. Once you learn that you can truly solve all your business and financial problems, you'll realize that the same approach can be used to address many of your personal problems as well. Even more importantly, by solving your business problems, by overcoming each and every obstacle on your path to career success, by repeatedly turning no into yes, your confidence will increase, your self-esteem will soar, and you will feel totally in charge of your own destiny. That's because success and failure build on themselves, both chemically and behaviorally.

Negative feelings suppress the production of chemicals in the brain called endorphins. A decrease in endorphins leads to feelings of depression. Depression then generates even more negative feelings, and you're stuck in a downward spiral toward the black pit of misery.

Positive feelings, on the other hand, like those you'll have after overcoming an obstacle or turning a no into a yes, increase the level of endorphins in the brain. That leads to a natural high that increases your resistance to pain and stress, and boosts your strength and stamina. Obviously, that natural high also generates more positive feelings, leading you up a positive climb toward happiness.

A person who is repeatedly unable to solve his business problems will also fall into a behavioral pattern that leads to even more failure. Someone who sees himself as a failure will act in ways that perpetuate his failing. He'll set goals he's unable to reach. He'll then pursue those goals halfheartedly, increasing his chance of failure, since he "knows" he's bound to fail anyway. When confronted with an ambiguous or mixed outcome he'll focus on the negative aspects of it, turning it into the failure he expected. He'll then attribute each new failure to something about himself or something outside of himself that he believes can't be changed, setting the stage for ever more failures.

Conversely, a person who believes she will succeed, who has learned to overcome obstacles and turn no into yes, will enter a behavioral pattern that leads to more successes. Someone who sees herself as a success will act in ways that perpetuate her success. She'll select clearly defined goals that require effort, but that are achievable. She'll work hard, increasing her chances of success, since she feels her efforts will pay off. If she comes face-to-face with an ambiguous situation she'll focus on the positive aspects of it, turning it into the success she expected. If confronted with failure she'll attribute it to things about herself she can change, or to external forces that will be different the next time. She'll continually set the stage for repeated successes.

She, and you, can insure repeated success by following my problem-solving approach. Realize that there's a sameness to all problems: they all contain a no. Determine what really is your problem. Make sure you're dealing with one problem at a time. Frame your problems rationally not emotionally. Become an expert. Create an environment of trust. And, if you need to, literally turn no into yes.

Learn to solve problems by applying the Turning No into Yes approach to your business life and you will become more successful, happy, and self-confident than you can every imagine. You will revolutionize your business, career, and even your personal life. And to start, all you need do is turn the page.

What's Your Problem?

3

It isn't that they can't see the solution.
It is that they can't see the problem.

G. K. Chesterton, Scandal of Father Brown

I never *tell* a client he might be mistaken about what is his problem. Can you imagine the response? An apparently successful entrepreneur came to me recently to discuss ways to finance the purchase of a new facility. He was looking to me for help in negotiating and financing the purchase. If, after speaking with him for thirty minutes, I told him his problem wasn't how to buy the new facility, it was that he needed to reinvent his business, he would have been out the door before I finished my sentence. Not only would I have lost a client, but I also would have missed a chance to be of help to someone who clearly needed assistance. Instead, I tried to *show* the client where his real problem was by asking a series of probing questions. I attempted to get the client to come to the realization himself. Of course, sometimes I can't do that—after all, I'm not a psychotherapist—and I'm eventually forced to spell out my insight and let the chips fall where they may.

With you, on the other hand, I think I can be a bit more direct. While you may have come to this book looking for help with a specific problem, as a reader you're approaching the topic more dispassionately than a client. You've spent only about a tenth of the cost of an hour with me, so you're probably willing to spend more time reading about my ideas than if you were sitting around my office table, listening to me while the meter was running. As a reader you've decided to make an investment of time rather than money, so you're less apt to get angry when confronted by a statement that could be perceived as criticism. At least that's my hope.

About one-third of the clients who come to my office are focusing on the wrong problem; they are concentrating on the wrong no. Some are fixated on a symptom rather than the malady. Others have locked onto the most obvious difficulty. A few concentrate on respectable, rather than potentially embarrassing, problems. Occasionally clients even take on the problems of others. Let me give you some examples.

SYMPTOMATIC RATHER THAN ROOT PROBLEM

I'm not a big sports fan, so when I saw the name Larry Peterson on my appointment calendar it didn't mean a thing to me. However, my assistant, Anthony, who loves basketball, could barely contain his excitement. Larry was a veteran forward with one of the local NBA teams. Anthony explained to me that Peterson was a solid, not flashy, player whose long career seemed at its end.

When Larry Peterson arrived in my office it was in the guise of a businessman, not a ballplayer. Even though he wore an Armani suit and carried a Seeger briefcase, they didn't hide his physical presence. A very tall muscular man with a shaved head that accentuated his chiseled features, Larry could barely squeeze into the chair in my outer office. Larry's attire was well chosen, since he had come to me for help in buying an auto dealership. It seems that his initial franchise application had been rejected, and Larry wanted my help in overcoming the rejection.

As always, I began the consultation by asking for an overview of Larry's entire financial life. The real problem was soon quite obvious. Larry's finances were run by a business manager who seemed more concerned with keeping Larry happy than financially secure. Larry had minority interests in a whole litany of businesses, some sound investments—like a chain of fast-food restaurants—others clear losers—such as the manufacturer of a line of tacky statuettes. Because of his varied holdings, Larry fancied himself an entrepreneur. Yet when I asked him about the operations, he didn't seem to know much besides the nature of the business and the name of his partners. All of Larry's paychecks and bills went to this manager's office. Applying for the auto dealership was Larry's first solo foray into business. He filled out the preliminary paperwork himself, assuming the routine credit investigation would be just that, routine. As you can guess, it wasn't.

While Larry initially came to me for help in overcoming his rejected application to buy an auto dealership, his real problem was that his finances were a shambles and that he had abdicated all personal responsibility for his money. The credit rejection was just a symptom of his true malady. The real no was his lack of control over his financial life.

MOST OBVIOUS RATHER THAN MOST IMPORTANT PROBLEM

Linda Birnbaum and Marilyn Jenrette were partners in a SoHo art gallery. Actually, they weren't really partners, and they thought that was the problem.

While the two women had been splitting the work and the profits fifty-fifty for more than a decade, the business was formally owned by Linda and her ex-live-in-lover, Paul McClary, a successful landscape photographer. Linda held seventy-five percent of the stock and Paul held twenty-five percent. Paul had never actually helped in the business, but in exchange for his putting up some seed money, Linda had given him one-quarter interest in the gallery. After Paul moved out, Linda hadn't bothered to buy him out, since there hadn't been any profits—she was struggling just to keep up with the rent. It wasn't until Marilyn, a college friend of Linda's, had come into the business that there were any profits to speak of.

From her first day in the gallery, Marilyn acted as, and was treated as, an equal partner. Together the two women built the business into a well-known and apparently lucrative business. Profits were put back into the business or split fifty-fifty. Paul never asked for nor expected anything from the profits. He was genuinely happy for Linda and Marilyn's success. This seemingly idyllic scene was only disturbed by the entrance of a man into Marilyn's life.

Marilyn's boyfriend (soon to be her husband) was concerned by the informal nature of the business. An attorney, he was worried that Marilyn's partnership status wasn't legally acknowledged. His legitimate concerns for Marilyn's well-being planted a seed that started eating at her. Marilyn voiced her fears to Linda, who, while understanding them on one level, was also hurt at what she perceived to be Marilyn's lack of trust. Linda was also disturbed by the thought of having to get back in touch with Paul and come up with money to buy him out.

For nearly two years the partnership issue remained unresolved. Superficially the business operated as before. However, there was a undercurrent of tension. Finally, I got a call from Marilyn's husband, who I had worked with on some other matters. I agreed to meet with the two women, help them clear up the situation, and then draft a partnership agreement.

When they arrived at my office there was an air of tension. I sat with them and got all the details of the partnership mess. Then, in an effort to start figuring out how to value the stock in the business, I started going over the gallery's financial information. Revenues were stagnant while expenses were climbing. Their lease was about to run out and would need to be renegotiated. In a nutshell, the business desperately needed to increase its revenues. I set the partnership issue aside and started asking Marilyn and Linda about how they planned to bring more money in; had they worked out a new marketing program, for instance? Once again, you can guess the answer.

The partnership issue had been so glaring and annoying that Linda and Marilyn had failed to see the business's real dilemma: it needed to boost revenues. The obvious ownership question would be moot if they didn't deal with the more pressing no: their revenue problem

RESPECTABLE, RATHER THAN EMBARRASSING, PROBLEM

Gloria Crenshaw came to see me at the urging of one of her friends, whose divorce I had helped mediate. Around seventy years old, petite, and very well mannered, Gloria made a refined entrance into my office late one Wednesday afternoon. Her clothes were elegant but worn. She was the epitome of shabby gentility. Gloria charmed my staff and then gracefully sat down in my office. She calmly explained to me that her ex-husband had called three weeks earlier to say he could no longer afford to send the monthly check she had been receiving for ten years. Without that check, she said, she would be impoverished.

Gloria's husband was a successful novelist. One of his books had become a very successful motion picture. Thanks to some savvy negotiating by his agent, he had been receiving substantial checks from the film for more than two decades. He and Gloria had been married for thirty years and had no children. In their divorce settlement, he had paid off and then given her their New York apartment: a huge five-bedroom place on Park Avenue. He had also agreed to make alimony payments, but had, in fact, been paying her twice the required amount. His recent call had been to say that he could no longer afford the extra funds and would simply be making the agreed-upon payment. Gloria had come to ask my help in getting her ex husband to change his mind and continue the larger payments. I explained to Gloria that before I called her ex-husband I'd need to take a look at her assets, liabilities, income, and expenses. She told me she would have her accountant send the information over the next day.

A package of materials arrived via messenger from Gloria's accountant the next afternoon. I was stunned by what I read. Gloria's apartment, which she owned, was worth well over $1 million. She had inherited an investment portfolio from her parents that was worth in excess of $3 million. Yet she truly didn't have enough money in her checking account to pay the monthly maintenance on her apartment. With a fortune in assets sitting unused, she really was depending on the monthly stipend sent along by her ex-husband.

When Gloria came back to my office that Friday I asked her about the discrepancy between her income and her assets. At first she was uncharacteristically indignant, saying I had no right to ask such questions. But when I told her I couldn't in all good conscience call her husband to ask for more money when she already had so much available to her, she began to cry. Through the sobs I was able to piece together the real story.

Gloria knew nothing about managing money. She didn't even know how to balance her checkbook. When she was young her father had handled things for her, then her husband took over their financial affairs. When he left she was too embarrassed by her ignorance to ask for any help. All she knew was that the check he sent was just enough to cover her bills.

Gloria's problem wasn't that she would be impoverished. The real no was that she didn't know how to handle the riches she really possessed, and was too embarrassed to let anyone know of her ignorance.

SOMEONE ELSE'S PROBLEM

Henrietta Sitney was a warm, sensitive older woman who looked like Golda Meir and sounded like Bella Abzug. She had come to see me at the insistence of her daughter Cheryl who, along with her husband and two children, lived in Northern California. Cheryl wanted Henrietta to leave New York and move west. Henrietta refused, saying she couldn't afford it.

Even though Henrietta's three-bedroom apartment on the Upper West Side of Manhattan was rent subsidized, the past two meager rent increases had brought her perilously close to the financial edge. Henrietta's husband, Max, had died twenty years ago, leaving her with a small life insurance settlement, his pension from his thirty years in the Meat Cutters Union, and his Social Security. At one time that fixed income had been enough to live a comfortable middle-class life in Manhattan. It wasn't any longer. On the other hand, she *could* live comfortably in Northern California. Cheryl had earlier sent me information on assisted living residences near her home in California. While she wouldn't be dining at Spago every night, Henrietta's money would certainly go further if she moved. Yet when I pointed this out to her, she refused to consider it.

Henrietta didn't live alone. Three years after her husband had died, her friend Jean's husband also died. The two couples had been inseparable. Jean's husband, Frank, was apparently a charming rogue. Though he always had enough to tip a bartender he never seemed to have enough to buy the kids new winter coats. He died leaving Jean with little more than his memory and some credit card bills. Henrietta didn't think twice about asking Jean to move into her apartment . . . and for the past seventeen years they had been roommates. Henrietta paid all the apartment-related bills herself, while Jean only paid half the food bill.

Henrietta's problem wasn't that she couldn't afford to move; it was that Jean couldn't afford to stay. Henrietta was taking Jean's problem as her own; she was confronting someone else's no.

WHY TRUE PROBLEMS ARE CONCEALED AND HOW THEY'RE REVEALED

My clients aren't unusual in their frequent inability to focus on their true problems. In fact, it's a common psychological phenomenon. People rarely discriminate among their problems. Generally, people lock onto whatever problem is right in front of them, whether it's real or imagined, important or minor. Their perception of that problem right in front of them can also be colored by old patterns of behavior and thought. It's an oversimplification, but someone whose father was emotionally abusive might be very quick to perceive their boss as abusive, whether or not that's the literal truth.

These initial complaints are what therapists call presenting problems, and they use them as indications of underlying problems. They see presenting problems as the tip of the psychological iceberg, as symptoms, or manifestations, of other, deeper difficulties. A good counselor will use the presenting problem as a signpost of possible paths to pursue in talk therapy. As one therapist told me, though presenting problems initially obscure the real problem from clients, eventually they enlighten the situation.

I'm not a psychotherapist. I have neither their training nor their time frame. Most of the people who come to my office are here because of a serious money problem. Something is wrong and it's so unbearable or potentially damaging that they need to act right away. As I noted earlier in this chapter, about two-thirds of the time, my clients are right about what is their real problem. When you've been turned down for a bank loan, most often that *is* your real problem. And generally it doesn't matter if the banker's rejection reminded you of the time your father wouldn't increase your allowance. But for those one-third of my clients who *aren't* focusing on their real problem, the potential for disaster is all too real. Just think of what would have happened to Marilyn and Linda if they'd continued to concentrate on negotiating a partnership agreement rather than on their gallery's finances. By the time their agreement was signed they'd have been equal owners of a bankrupt business.

Focusing on the wrong no is wasted effort. Even if you succeed in turning that no around, you'll be no closer to success than when you first started, you'll have lost time, and you'll be frustrated and depressed. You'll have achieved a Pyrrhic victory: one so costly it might as well be a defeat.

Because I need to move quickly to determine a client's real need, and because, as a legal and financial advisor, I'm less concerned with the deep-seated reasons for a problem than I am with the problem itself, I use a very aggressive initial approach when questioning my clients. I probe both personal and business finances. I generally look at business plans, marketing plans, budgets, forecasts, balance sheets, profit and loss statements, tax returns, accounts receivable and payable statements, and cash flow statements. I often have clients do intensive salary surveys, prepare scripts for conversations, or track their spending. And I always ask lots of specific questions and some very pointed hypothetical questions.

Remember that entrepreneur I described in the beginning of this chapter—the fellow who came to me for help in buying a new facility? The key to getting him to realize his real problem was to ask just such a hypothetical question. All I did was ask him, "If you were going to pick a business to go into today, would it be the one you're in?" He didn't say anything for about thirty seconds. He just stared out my office window. And if you've been in my office you'd know it wasn't because the view is entrancing. Finally he turned and looked me in the eye. "No," was all he said. A small word, but it represented quite an epiphany for him. When we began to discuss his answer we discovered his desire to buy a new facility was really an effort to inject some creativity into what had become a stale business. His problem wasn't that he needed to buy new space, it was that he needed to reinvent his business.

HOW YOU CAN UNCOVER YOUR OWN REAL PROBLEM

A psychotherapist is trained to dig behind presenting problems by asking leading questions. I've learned to uncover the real no by looking at financial documents and asking pointed questions. But neither therapists nor I try to practice this technique on ourselves. How then can you uncover your own real problems? There are three ways.

First, you can always speak to a therapist or contact me if you have the money or inclination.* I'm using the word *therapist* in a looser manner than it's commonly applied. If you have what you perceive to be a personal finance problem, I'd suggest using as your therapist a fee-only financial planner (one who charges by the hour rather than taking a commission on sales) with whom you feel some rapport. If you perceive your problem to be business related, I'd look for a small-business consultant to be your therapist, finding one through the chamber of commerce, the nearest SBA office, your state's small-business development center, the local office of the Service Corps of

---

*Seriously, I'd be happy to correspond or chat with any reader. You can reach me online at mark4smp@aol.com or you can write to me care of HarperCollins.

Retired Executives (SCORE), or your trade association. If you perceive you have a career problem, you can ask your professional team if they can recommend any career counselors to serve as your therapist. If they don't know of any candidates, contact the career and placement offices at the largest local college and ask for names.

Second, if you have the time you could also start writing about your problems in a journal. Writing about issues often provides sufficient distance to see things clearly. Take out a legal pad or notebook and begin describing your situation. Write down your fears and worries, as well as your goals and dreams. Describe what you think will happen if you fail and what you believe will happen if you succeed. Then, put the pad or notebook away for at least twenty-four hours. After a day's reflection, read what you'd written. Does it make sense? Do your fears accurately reflect reality, or are they exaggerated? Viewed objectively, on the page, does it seem that you're focusing on the right problem?

Having written this book, it's obvious I don't think it's always necessary to speak with a therapist or someone like me. And, unless you have a rare gift for self-analysis, even months of journal writing might not lead to a breakthrough. That's why I think the third technique is the best way for you to uncover your true problems: find yourself some problem mentors. Actually, you probably already have them, and you simply need to start using them more often.

Don't you ask your spouse or a sibling for advice on dealing with your mother? Haven't you gone to a friend for suggestions on a problem you're having with your wife or husband? When you were thinking about buying a home, didn't you ask your parents for their opinions? Do you have a group of coworkers you rely on for help in navigating office politics? Are you often calling your mentors for suggestions about career directions? Before you make business decisions do you speak with your partner, lawyer, accountant, or your friend who runs a similar operation?

Obviously the answer to all these questions is yes. We each have an entire network of people we go to for help with our personal and business problems. Generally, however, we only turn to them for help in making decisions. My suggestion is that you turn to your network of problem mentors much earlier. Rather than asking them for opinions on how to solve your problem, ask them for opinions on what really is your problem. And listen closely. They are invariably right.

Problem mentors can uncover true problems so effectively because they have a fresh, unbiased perspective on your problem. Problem mentors *can* discriminate among your problems. None of your problems are right in front of them, so they're not going to automatically lock onto whatever problem is most obvious. Since they're not bringing the same emotional or psychological baggage to the issue as you are, they're going to be able to tell whether a problem is real or imagined, important or minor. Since it's your problem, not their own, their perceptions of your problem won't be influenced by your patterns of behavior and thought.

The next time you feel you have a problem, turn to someone who knows you and whose opinion you trust. Tell her the facts. Explain what you're feeling. And then ask her what she thinks your problem is. If she agrees with your analysis, that's great. If she doesn't, listen closely to what she says. She's probably right. In either case you'll have figured out your real no.

I need to offer one caveat, however. It can be a mistake to use your spouse or lover as a sounding board for problems with which he or she is also involved. Couples tend to naturally polarize. If one is a neat freak, the other will become a slob. If one is a spendthrift, the other will become a miser. If one is compulsively early, the other will become compulsively late. Obviously, this polarizing needn't be as extreme as I've portrayed it, nor does it need to be consistent (the neat freak in the house could be the slob in the car). Still, it happens to nearly every couple. This can cause difficulties in problem solving. Your partner might not be able to overcome his or her natural tendency toward balancing you and be able to give you an unbiased analysis. That's why it makes sense for your mate to be one of your business problem mentors, but perhaps not one of your personal problem mentors.

OVERCOMING THEIR REAL PROBLEMS

Before you move on to the next item, let me fill you in on what happened to the clients whose stories I've mentioned in this chapter.

Larry Peterson, the professional basketball player, came to me for help buying an auto dealership, when his real problem was that he had abdicated all personal responsibility for his money. After a great deal of indecision, Larry fired the business manager who had led him to the brink of financial ruin. I helped him find an accountant and financial planner to clean up his financial life and teach him how to handle his own money. Larry stopped playing entrepreneur and, upon his retirement from the NBA, found a job doing something he knew: being a television commentator for basketball games. After two years in television Larry took a job as an assistant coach. He then moved into the front office of the team and became assistant general manager.

Linda Birnbaum and Marilyn Jenrette, the art gallery owners, had come to me for help in cleaning up ownership issues, when their real problem was that the business was starving for more revenue. When I pointed out how dire their business finances really were, Linda and Marilyn instantly set aside the issues that had divided them. They launched a successful new marketing plan and within six months had recruited a handful of new artists, one of whom, a sculptor who makes somewhat disturbing life-size statues of himself, has become quite popular. Once the business was on a surer foundation, Linda met with her ex-husband, Paul, who was happy to sell his shares for little more than his initial investment. Marilyn bought Paul's twenty-five percent share, and another twenty-five percent from Linda, and today they are equal partners, formally as well as practically.

Gloria Crenshaw had come to me with the fear of being impoverished, but she actually was too embarrassed to let anyone know her financial ignorance. In order to help Gloria overcome her embarrassment I had her meet with a very down-to-earth female financial planner I'd worked with in the past. The planner had the patience to take Gloria step by step through all the adjustments she needed to make in her finances in order to become independent. Gloria has sold the Park Avenue apartment and used the proceeds to buy a smaller but still lovely apartment in Florida. The planner has also revamped Gloria's investment portfolio so it generates sufficient income for her to live comfortably.

Henrietta Sitney had believed she couldn't afford to move, when actually the problem was that her roommate, Jean, couldn't afford to stay in the apartment without her. This was actually the toughest of all four problems to overcome. Henrietta's daughter Cheryl and I worked very hard at trying to get Henrietta to see that she had to put herself first; that, in fact, she had no choice, since she wouldn't be able to afford the apartment any longer. We had very little success. It was actually Jean who finally turned Henrietta around. After a long talk with Cheryl, Jean called her nephew in Oregon and arranged to move into an adult home near his house, freeing Henrietta from her perceived obligation. Henrietta now lives in an adult community in California, ten minutes from Cheryl's house.

One Problem at a Time $\quad$ **4**

The best way to eat the elephant standing in your path
is to cut it up into little pieces.

African proverb

Problems are like teenagers: though they often gather in packs, they're
easier to deal with separately.

Many clients who come to my office saying they need help in solving a problem are actually facing a series or cluster of related problems. When they sit down across from me they say, "I hate my job," or
"I need help organizing my financial life," or "I don't know what to do
about my business." Invariably, these clients come to me because
they're either frustrated at their inability to solve (or perhaps even
address) their problem, or they've repeatedly failed and don't know
why.

I try to patiently explain that the source of their frustration and
their repeated failures is that they're trying to act like Superman and
leap a tall building in a single bound; they're trying to get from the
starting line to the finish tape in one stride; they're trying to turn a
dozen different nos into a single yes. Is it any wonder they're falling
short or falling down. They need to learn the second item in the Turning No into Yes program: make sure you're dealing with one no at a
time.

One of the truisms of problem solving is that the more specific your problem, the easier it is to solve. Another truism is that once you get on a roll of solving your problems, your confidence builds and your problem-solving skills improve even more. In other words, take lots of small steps and you will eventually get to the finish line.

Sounds simple, doesn't it? Well, when you have a legal and financial consultant sitting across the table from you who can quickly diagnose the situation, isolate the specific individual problems, and then prioritize them, it *is* relatively easy to change your focus. But since you're not sitting across the desk from me you're going to have to do a bit more work than my clients. You need to first figure out if you're fixating on a big picture, rather than focusing on, and solving, the individual pixel problems that make it up. Then, you need to decide whether you should prioritize those smaller problems, or address them chronologically. Before I get into the details, let's look at two instances when clients of mine were fixated on the big picture.

OVERWHELMED BY DECISIONS

Wendy Levin, a sixty-two-year-old widow with a lovely smile, was sent to me by her son, Mitchell, a colleague of mine, who had grown frustrated at trying to help his mother sort out and address her financial problems.

For most of her life, Wendy had someone else around to take care of her finances. She had lived with her parents until her marriage to Elliot Levin at age eighteen. Up until then, Wendy simply handed her paycheck to her father, who handled the family finances. After marriage, Elliot, who doted on her, took over the job. When they left their rental apartment in Brooklyn to move to a house they had bought in suburban Long Island, it was because Elliot said it was time. He handled all the details. Even after Wendy went back into the workforce when their son Mitchell entered high school, she continued to rely entirely on Elliot. At the end of the week, Wendy handed the check she received for doing secretarial work for a small manufacturer over to Elliot. He, in turn, handed her enough cash to buy groceries and take care of the household needs. If work needed to be done around the house, or if Wendy wanted to buy a new outfit, she asked Elliot if they could afford it. He'd either say yes or no, and she would respond accordingly. They lived a happy, traditional, middle-class suburban life until Elliot dropped dead from a heart attack one morning while waiting for his commuter train.

Aside from the grief and psychological upheaval, Wendy was in a financial quandary. Elliot hadn't left her destitute—there was his pension, their joint savings, and a life insurance benefit. Sure, Wendy still needed to work at her job, but she didn't need to change her lifestyle immediately. Wendy's dilemma was that she didn't know the first thing about personal finance. She had never even paid the bills. For the first few months, Mitchell handled the financial matters for her. He also steered her toward a tax preparer, insurance broker, and investment advisor. After two years Wendy was able to run her own money life with the help of her professionals and with only the occasional question for Mitchell.

That changed when the company she worked for was bought out by a larger competitor. In an effort to avoid layoffs, the new company offered Wendy and some of the other older employees an early retirement package. Suddenly, Wendy was faced with another upheaval. There was no question that she'd have to take the package, since the alternative was probably termination. But what would she do then? Stay in, or leave, the workforce? Stay in, or sell, her house? Stay in, or leave, New York? All these issues rolled into one large problem for Wendy: "What should I do?" she repeatedly asked Mitchell. Mitchell would respond by asking, "What do you want to do?" At which point Wendy would cry and say she didn't know.

With no experience at making major life decisions, Wendy was unable to break her situation down into smaller, more manageable pieces. Mitchell, understandably unwilling to make decisions for her, was frustrated by her indecision. That's when he sent her to me.

THE CLASSIC NEW YORK CATCH-22

Ken and Mary Schoenfeld* look like they've stepped right out of the film *The Big Chill*. Ken, forty-four, looks like the actor Kevin Kline, while Mary, forty, resembles Glenn Close.

Ken, a native New Yorker, has had a meteoric rise in the advertising industry. Leaving college with a degree in English he landed a job as a junior account executive at a small agency. He was lucky, or savvy

---

*Readers of *Die Broke* might remember Ken and Mary from that book.

enough, to concentrate his efforts on the then fledgling computer industry. Ken hopped from agency to agency, each time getting a jump in pay and responsibility. By the time he came to see me he was creative director at a medium-size agency and was earning a little over $300,000 a year.

Mary, who was born in a suburb of Chicago and who studied photography in college, came to New York after graduation to serve as an assistant to a well-known fashion photographer. After a five-year apprenticeship she went into business on her own. She met Ken when they worked on an ad campaign together. After their marriage and the birth of their first child—Juliet—Mary shifted her focus to product photography, since it didn't require travel. Of course, it did require a large studio space. They were lucky enough to find a large and affordable (for New York City) loft space downtown. In fact, the space was large enough that when they got pregnant again two years after Juliet's birth, they were able to create yet another room for their second child, Penelope.

Ken and Mary lived out the "yuppie" fantasy. Ken bought new clothes weekly, rationalizing his expensive wardrobe as a cost of doing business. Mary had a similar wardrobe in order to "look right" on Ken's arm when they went out with his clients. And the girls, even though they never met clients, were just as well dressed. Of course, it wasn't just clothes. Ken and Mary had dined out nearly every night before they'd had children, and after that they had become take-out fanatics. The family went on luxury vacations. They also furnished and refurnished the loft.

But when Mary tried to get back to work full-time a couple of months after Penelope's birth, cracks started appearing in their carefully sculpted life. It was easier finding space in their loft for a second child than it was finding time in their schedules. Even though she worked from home Mary soon realized she'd need help if she was going to continue working full-time. After some failed attempts at getting day help they realized they'd need to find a live-in nanny and, as a result, a larger home.*

---

*I realize that some readers may view Ken and Mary's problem as one they'd love to have. While theirs was what I call a top shelf problem, it was nevertheless still a problem. As I wrote in chapter 1, my role is to solve my clients' problems whether they're life threatening or annoying, real or imagined. I didn't judge Ken and Mary's problem . . . and I won't judge yours.

Ken and Mary needed sufficient space for two children (they didn't plan on having any more), a live-in nanny, themselves, and Mary's business. They wanted to be near enough to Manhattan so Ken wouldn't spend more time commuting than with the kids, yet they wanted a safe area with good schools.

After just a couple of months of searching, they came to see me. Ken and Mary said their problem was that they were trapped by their own success. They'd looked at larger places and simply couldn't figure out how they'd be able to pay for a live-in nanny and the larger home. Of course, if Mary stopped working they wouldn't need the nanny or the larger place, but without Mary's income they couldn't even afford the place they were in now. Ken called their situation "the classic New York catch-22."

THE SINGLE ACTION TEST

I could immediately tell that Wendy as well as Ken and Mary weren't focusing on individual specific problems. That's because I applied my "single action" test to their situations. If a client is focusing on a problem that cannot be resolved by taking a single realistic action (winning the lottery doesn't count), then they're focusing too widely. Similarly, if a problem can't be solved with a single yes, it's really a cluster or series of nos.

If you come to me and say "I hate my job," there's no one single action you or I can take that would solve the situation. Instead, we'd need to start breaking the issue down into smaller chunks until we found a problem that could be solved with one action. For instance, we'd have to find out why you hate your job. Let's say you realized you hate your job because you're not making enough money, or because your boss is nasty. In those cases we could solve the problem with one action—getting a raise, or getting a new job in the same industry. However, if you discovered you hate your job because you no longer find your industry rewarding, then we would need to keep digging further to find out more and to eventually get to a problem we could solve with a single action.

Wendy couldn't resolve her situation by taking one action. She was facing a series of problems: should she retire or look for another job? If she retired, did she want to stay in New York or move? If she wanted to stay in New York could she afford to continue living in her house?

If she wanted to move, where would she go? And on and on. I could also see that Wendy's inexperience at decision making was leading her to look at the big picture and, as a result, become paralyzed with indecision. Wendy needed to address specific individual problems first. That way she could make smaller decisions of the type she *did* have experience making.

Ken and Mary couldn't cure their stated problem with one action either. Ken unknowingly acknowledged that when he referred to their situation as a catch-22. Considering they already had a combined income of anywhere from $400,000 to $600,000 a year, depending on how well Mary's business did, it seemed unlikely money was their problem. Once I started digging into their expenses I found that Ken and Mary had accumulated more than $75,000 in credit card debt and were making minimum payments each month of $2,000. With an income that averaged about half a million dollars a year they had no savings. In addition, they had no financial plans for providing for their children. And Mary had no business plan. They were leading an ad hoc life. They needed to take charge of their personal and business lives, and that can only be done one step at a time.

If your problem cannot be solved by taking one, realistic action, then you're trying to be Superman. You're also setting yourself up for failure. No matter how much energy and intelligence you may have, you can only do one thing well at a time. Try to do more than one thing and you insure you'll do none of them well. This is one instance when it's best to set your sights low . . . that way you guarantee you'll hit the target.

SERIES OR CLUSTER?

If you've uncovered that you're focusing on too big a picture and need to narrow your vision, you next need to decide how to break that big dilemma down into smaller, specific problems. There are two approaches you can take. If your situation is actually a series of problems, then you need to deal with them in a logical chronological order. If your situation is actually a cluster of related, but nonsequential problems, then you need to prioritize them and deal with the most important first.

You can tell you have a series of problems if they naturally fall into a linear pattern. If you can picture your problems as a row of dominoes falling, one into another, then you're facing a series. For instance, Wendy needed first to decide whether or not she wanted to retire. That would affect whether she wanted to remain in her house. And that would help her decide where she would live.

You can tell you have a cluster of problems if they are all connected, but in no particular order. If you can picture your problems as individual doors surrounding you in a circle, then you're facing a cluster. For example, Ken and Mary had to get a handle on their spending, decide on their child care options, figure out their real estate needs, establish a savings and investment plan, and work out business and career plans. All were related, but not in a clearly sequential order.

FACING A SERIES OF PROBLEMS

If you determine you're facing a series of problems, you need to figure out which problem to address first. Obviously, if one problem is clearly the trigger, setting the rest of the series in motion, it should be addressed first. In cases where it's not so obvious, look for the problem that has the shortest deadline.

The first thing Wendy and I went over was whether or not she wanted to retire. That was clearly her first domino. All the other subsequent decisions were contingent on that one. Fortunately, this was an easy decision for Wendy. She had never really enjoyed her job: it was a reason to get out of the house and generate a stream of income, nothing more. Wendy decided to accept the retirement package.

After addressing the trigger problem, the others in a series often naturally fall into sequence.

Next, Wendy and I looked at whether she wanted to remain in her house. She loved her home, but the four-bedroom split level was far more house than she needed. Wendy came home, ate dinner, and then retired to her bedroom to watch television. She might as well be living in a one-bedroom apartment. The taxes were high, and she had to pay for a gardener during the summer and a snowplow service in the winter. Before we even looked into the financial ramifications of staying, Wendy reached the decision to sell.

She was just starting to get frightened about selling her home, almost losing her focus on specifics, when I steered her instead to the question of where she would like to relocate. Wendy's son Mitchell and his family had bought a house in another New York suburb. And she had friends who were planning on staying in New York for at least another ten years. But she also had friends in Florida and loved the warm weather and relaxed lifestyle. I encouraged her to go down to Florida for a visit and to also start looking around her current area to see what smaller homes would cost. When I next saw her she had reached a decision: she would get more for her money in Florida and she thought she'd lead a fuller life. She would move to the Sunbelt.

With that decision made, Wendy and I started discussing real estate. I explained to her that in her situation it made more sense to sell first and buy second. If she sold quickly she could always rent an affordable place in Florida until she found a place to buy. I encouraged her to rely on a savvy real estate broker I knew and to let me help with the negotiating. Meanwhile, I suggested she make another visit to Florida to look around.

Wendy's home sold within three months for $225,000, a bit less than she wanted but still quite an increase from the $25,000 she and her husband paid for it thirty years earlier. While the deal was being closed, Wendy called me to say she'd found a place in Florida that she liked.

Othello Woods was a very large, multiphase development just outside Boca Raton. Wendy had friends living there and liked the community. The final phase of construction was under way: two four-story apartment buildings, and a block of attached single family homes. The less expensive apartments were more to Wendy's taste and budget. She put down a deposit. The sales agent helped her find a rental unit in the same development so she could move down after we closed the sale of her home in New York. Four months after moving down to Florida, Wendy was in her new apartment.

DEALING WITH CLUSTER PROBLEMS

Since there's no clear trigger problem in a cluster, one good method for sorting the individual problems is by priority. Ask yourself which problem presents the greatest immediate danger, or which is causing the most pain or difficulty. For instance, if you need to redirect your business, it makes sense before you sit down and develop a new marketing plan to work out a deal with the landlord who's clamoring for back rent.

If there isn't one problem that's clearly the most dangerous, or is causing the most pain or difficulty, I suggest you look to see if there's one fundamental or keystone problem all the others rest on. For example, if all your financial problems stem from your spending too much money on luxury items, begin by stopping your discretionary spending. Even if that is the most difficult problem in the cluster, it makes sense to tackle it first, because solving it may result in the other problems vanishing or shrinking dramatically.

Finally, if there's no clear trigger problem, no problem that's clearly the most threatening, and no keystone problem all the others rest on, I suggest you start by working on the easiest problem. Since you already perceive it to be the easiest, you'll be less likely to procrastinate. And if it really is the easiest, you'll solve it quickly and, as a result, boost your confidence for tackling the next one.

Once I had a chance to go over the cluster of problems facing Ken and Mary Schoenfeld, we decided to tackle their spending problems first. I believed their overspending held the most potential danger. It was also, actually, the easiest to solve, since it was totally in their control. Ken and Mary didn't see it that way, however.

We began by having Ken and Mary keep a month-long record of every penny they spent. I then asked them to swear off using their credit cards and to instead pay cash or write a check for all their expenses.* That added an element of awareness and perhaps even pain to each purchase. I gave them some consumer-oriented books so they could learn some shopping skills. Whenever they balked I told them to take a look at their two daughters and ask themselves if they'd rather spend the $14 on them or a gourmet sandwich. While Ken and Mary were never going to become ascetics they stopped being wastrels.

Next we examined their child care situation because we agreed that it was now their most pressing problem. Since there was no acceptable and affordable day care in their area, and since Mary couldn't work and care for both girls, the choice came down to hiring a full-time nanny or Mary giving up her career temporarily. After some preliminary investigations it was clear that Mary made far more than was needed to pay for an acceptable nanny. Besides, Mary didn't want to give up her career, even temporarily. She and Ken believed, and I came to

---

*My work with Ken and Mary on their spending habits is fully explored in *Die Broke*.

agree with them, that if she was out of the business for even as short as three years she would have to start over from scratch.

With a nanny on the way, Ken and Mary had to examine their real estate situation. They needed more space, but a larger loft in the same or a similar Manhattan neighborhood was more than they could afford. After looking at homes in the suburbs, and investigating buying a smaller apartment while also renting studio space for Mary, they decided to make some compromises. They chose to move out of Manhattan and into an up-and-coming, formerly industrial part of Queens. There they could buy for less money a larger loft space than they had now. They wouldn't be in as chic a neighborhood, and Ken could no longer walk to his office, but Mary could still work at home and be close to the kids . . . and the nanny. They were even able to take some of the money they made from the sale of their Manhattan loft and use it to pay down their credit card bills.

With those three short-term problems solved we could turn to longer-term issues: career and business plans, and savings and investment plans. Mary was quite happy being in business for herself. She knew, however, that professional photography could be a capricious business. Ken laughed when he heard that, saying advertising made photography seem secure. Ken said he'd love having the kind of control over his work that Mary had. After a few minutes of banter they'd come up with the germ of a business: they'd eventually form their own small agency, specializing at first in the computer industry. It seemed the perfect meshing of Mary's skills and Ken's contacts. They began putting their ideas down on paper.

Finally, Ken, Mary, and I turned toward at least contemplating a savings and investment plan. With their spending under control and their real estate costs lowered, they could see a light at the end of the financial tunnel. Once Penelope, their youngest, was in school, Ken and Mary agreed they'd be able to devote the money now spent on their nanny to their future. And now that they had the dream of starting their own business, they had yet another reason to follow through on the savings and investment plan.

ONE STEP AT A TIME

Wendy Levin had never made a major life decision. Confronted with a major life crossroads, her lack of knowledge and experience led her to see her situation as a single, unsolvable problem. But by getting some help in breaking down that huge, seemingly unscalable problem into smaller, specific problems, and then by addressing them chronologically, Wendy not only made major life decisions but also made them well.

Ken and Mary Schoenfeld were leading an ad hoc life. Buffeted by a cluster of financial and lifestyle problems, their lack of focus had them thinking they were trapped by one gigantic catch-22 dilemma. But by separating out the individual threads that were snaring them, and then prioritizing them, they were able to completely solve most, and get started solving the others. Ken and Mary went from leading a haphazard life to being fully in charge and control of their present and future.

When you find yourself facing what seems to be an insurmountable hurdle, look again. Odds are it's really a number of hurdles, stacked one on top of the other. Unstack them, line them up sequentially or by priority, and jump them one at a time. You'll soon be at the finish line, a winner.

Focus on Facts, Not Feelings

5

When angry, count ten before you speak;
if very angry, an hundred.

Thomas Jefferson

I wish I could say my approach can be used to turn every no into a yes, to solve every problem you might have. But I can't. My approach can solve every *rational* problem and turn every *reasoned* no into a yes. It can't solve irrational problems or turn an emotional no into yes. By their very nature, emotional problems can't be solved through the application of facts and logic. Pretending otherwise is a big mistake.

Let me give you an example. Let's say you're deeply in love with someone who doesn't feel the same about you. They say that, while they love you (like a friend), they're not *in* love with you. That's the ultimate emotional no. Can you try to turn that no around? Sure; the attempt is made all the time. Throughout the ages people have tried to make someone else love them. But no matter how many flowers are sent, how many diamonds are bought, how many wonderful meals are cooked, or, to put it bluntly, how many sexual favors are offered, the attempt is always futile. The person making the effort ends up demeaning himself or herself. The object of desire sees the effort as pitiful, loses respect for the pursuer, and feels guilty. The pursuer loses self-respect, feels foolish, and often ends up hating the one he or she loved. Both parties end up feeling worse about themselves and each other.

Luckily, business or financial problems are always based in rational thinking and therefore can always be solved. But that doesn't mean clients don't come to my office and present what appear to be emotional problems. They do. Quite often actually. It's that they're actually casting a rational problem in an emotional light. Let me explain. Just as emotional problems are, by their nature, irrational, since they deal with feelings, so business and financial problems are, by their nature, rational, since they deal with facts and figures.

If you're facing a business or financial situation and you're focusing on feelings rather than figures, you're framing it in the wrong manner. In order to solve your problem, and turn that no into a yes, you need to strip the emotions from the situation and deal with your business obstacle rationally.

Don't feel bad about emotionalizing business problems. I do it all the time too. Even though I consciously know better, I often let my personal baggage get added onto a business obstacle. Sometimes I let my lifelong (hereditary) fears about money start to impact how I look at a pending deal. There are other times I let my expectations of how I think other people *should* do something affect my feelings about what they have done. At least once a week I find myself exposing a festering problem to the light of rationality and freeing myself of the emotional shadows I've cast on it.

After having done this for clients and myself for so long, I've developed a couple of simple techniques: counting to ten and listing examples. Which of these two techniques you use to shift from an emotional to a rational approach to a problem depends on how you fell into the trap in the first place. Clients generally get snared by their emotions for one of two reasons: either they're reacting too quickly to a problem, or they've let a problem sit too long and it has started to fester. Let's take a look at a couple of examples.

REACTING TOO QUICKLY

One Tuesday morning I got a telephone call from one of New York's most successful real estate brokers. She asked me if I had time later that day to hold an emergency consultation. I did, but when I started to ask for more information, the broker begged me not to ask any questions. I agreed. Three hours later the doorbell to my office rang. It was the broker, acting as if she had just robbed a bank and was looking for a hideout. She muttered a few words to my assistant, Anthony, just inside the doorway, and then ushered a short but wiry young man, wearing a black leather jacket, a bandanna on his head, and a pair of mirror sunglasses, into my private office. He also looked as if he was trying to hide . . . and he was. Just a week earlier his face had been on the cover of *People*.

Liam Adams spent his early twenties as a television star. A fresh-faced, intense young man, he had charmed his way into America's heart with a costarring role on a long-running drama. After ten years Liam left the show, despite its continuing success, in a much publicized effort to "stretch his acting wings." Despite the tart comments of many, Liam successfully made the jump to feature films. He starred in a number of commercially successful films, playing characters similar to the one he had made famous on television. By the time he came to see me, the charismatic thirty-five-year-old was trying to navigate the next shift in his career, from movie star to actor. He had just gotten rave reviews for his performance in a gritty low-budget love story.

As part of this continuing metamorphosis Liam was looking to buy an apartment in New York City so he could work in the theater more often. Unfortunately, the cover story in *People*, which had documented his acting efforts, had also talked of his real estate plans. That accounted for his stealthy garb when he showed up at my office. The reason for his being there was somewhat less stealthy: the broker had brought Liam to see me for an emergency consultation because earlier that morning he had been rejected by the coop board of one of New York's most famous apartment buildings. She had convinced a reluctant Liam to see me with promises that I could turn the situation around.

After putting him at ease about my office's discretion, I asked Liam what happened with the coop board. His mood and personality took a dramatic turn. Liam instantly shifted from shy and laconic to boisterous and profane. By listening through the curses, and concentrating on the broker's stammered interjections, I figured out that the coop board had asked Liam a series of what he deemed highly personal and inappropriate questions. Liam then told them what they could do with their questions, and they suggested he look for another apartment.

Once all the facts were on the table Liam became modest and sub-dued again. With evident embarrassment he apologized to me for his outburst. Liam explained that he had always had a quick temper, and with the added pressure of press attention his short fuse had gotten even shorter. Obviously, that had been part of the problem earlier in the day. Liam's highly developed sense of privacy and explosive temper had come up against a coop board's annoying but entirely legitimate quest for financial and personal information before approving a new member. I told Liam that I could help him turn the coop board's no into a yes.

LETTING PROBLEMS FESTER

Martin Jackson contacted me via E-mail after reading one of my books, *Live Rich*. A fifty-three-year-old chemical engineer, he had put in more than thirty years working for the same corporation: a midwestern-based multinational. Martin wrote to me for career advice. I don't think it's possible to conduct a consultation in cyberspace, so I arranged to have a telephone conversation with Martin over the weekend.

That Saturday, Martin told me his story. After earning his degree from a large university on the West Coast, Martin had been recruited to work for what was then a respected midsize company. During his first two decades with the company, Martin was on the fast track. So was the company. He earned a master's and doctorate on company time. Promotions and sizable salary increases came with regularity. Martin received regular calls from headhunters but always brushed them off, believing he had a big future with his company. Then, just about when he hit his midforties, his career seemed to derail.

Martin had always seen himself as a scientist first, and a business-man second. And for years that approach was encouraged by the com-pany. Then, in the early 1980s the company started changing. A well-known billionaire investor bought a large stake in the company and pushed for a new management team. That new team brought in new priorities. Innovation and technological advancements started taking a backseat to profits and stock values. He was told by some of his old mentors that to rise above the level where he had become stuck, he would need to shift his orientation. Martin, though a com-pany man through and through, wouldn't hear it. He still believed that somehow the old values would prevail. He was a true believer.

For ten years Martin continued to excel in his field, making major technological breakthroughs that led to notoriety and profits for the company. Martin published dozens of academic papers in respected journals. He lectured at university campuses and was sought out as an expert by government agencies. Yet he remained at the same level. His only raises were annual cost-of-living increases.

By the time he contacted me, Martin was bitter. He had loved the company too much not to now hate it.* All the resentment, anger, and frustration of the past decade had understandably hardened Martin's heart. After commiserating with him, and assuring him he wasn't alone—that corporate loyalty had died a near universal death, and it had nothing to do with him personally—I asked what I could do for him; what did he want from the company. His response was one word: respect. Hearing that, I knew we'd need more than just a telephone call to work things out.

THE WINDOW OF RATIONALITY

React too quickly to a business situation and you're apt to frame it in an emotional rather than rational manner. React too slowly and you're likely to do the same. The secret is to act within, what I call, the window of rationality. Give yourself sufficient time to think before you react to a problem, but then definitely take the action.

When Liam Adams got angry at the probing of the coop board and lashed out at them it was because he reacted too quickly. Anger, like Liam's, is the most common reflexive response to a business problem. Most of my clients who react this way do so because one of their "hot buttons" has been pushed. For whatever reason, a problem has touched on a sensitive area, and reflexively they lash out; it's like the fight-or-flight reflex.

Often, the area is so sensitive that the reaction is far more dramatic than was necessary. For instance, there are still times when someone in my office will say or do something that, while it appears innocuous to the rest of the world, will instantly make my blood boil. That's because I'm not actually responding to what he or she said or did; I'm responding to a whole history of similar situations. Liam Adams

---

*With apologies to Jean Racine, who wrote, "I loved him too much not to hate him at all."

snapped at the coop board, not just because of their questions but also in response to years of intrusions into his personal life.

We are human beings not computers, so we're always going to have emotions and our own sore spots. How then do we avoid reacting too quickly and treating a rational problem in an emotional manner? By counting to ten.

Really. Most times that's all it takes. Ironically, I've found that the more irrational the response, the less time it takes for it to pass. Rather than reflexively responding to a situation, give yourself time to think. If necessary, ask for some time to mull things over. There's nothing wrong with rationalizing the request if you need to save face. Tell the other party you need to speak to your partner, or consult your spouse, or check your appointment calendar, or double-check your figures. Just give yourself a chance to calm down, to set your emotions aside, and look at the situation rationally.

If you've already reacted too quickly to a problem, it's too late to count to ten. Instead, you need to remove the emotion from the environment. The best way to do that, ironically, isn't with a factual argument, but to make an appeal to the other party's emotions. In a word: apologize. Explain the personal circumstances that led to your outburst, say how sorry you are to have injected emotions into the mix, and then immediately respond rationally. I've found that humility works wonders in business situations . . . probably because it's so rare.

Martin Jackson reacted too slowly to his business problem. He let his frustrations with his company fester for ten years, so that when he finally expressed them it was as an emotional problem: the lack of respect.

Most of my clients who delay too long, do so because they hope the problem will go away by itself. Either they're afraid of dealing with the problem for some reason, or they find the potential solution so troublesome that they procrastinate. Unfortunately, problems are like weeds: they do not just go away. If you don't kill them, or at least contain them, they will grow larger and take over your business, career, or life. As time goes on and the problem fails to go away you get annoyed, first at the problem, and then eventually at yourself for having let it go on for so long. The annoyance becomes anger. Finally, having repressed your anger for as long as possible, something happens—often quite minor—that makes you snap.

Obviously, you can keep from letting problems fester by resolving to deal with them as soon as they crop up. You'll find that's easier to do once you've mastered the approach in this book. When you know you can solve any business problem by following my six-item checklist, you'll be far less apt to procrastinate.

If you've already waited too long to react and, as a result, have framed your problem emotionally rather than rationally, there's still hope. Set your emotions aside for a moment. Sit down at your desk, take out paper and pen, and draft a list of examples. Act as if you were preparing a memo to argue your case. Prioritize your examples from clearest to most tenuous. Stand up and stretch. Sit down again and pick up your list. This time, view those prioritized items, not as examples of an emotional problem, but as individual rational problems. Now, tackle the first one on the list.

LIAM AND MARTIN SET ASIDE THEIR EMOTIONS

After Liam Adams apologized to me for his outburst in my office, I asked him if he could apologize again. He looked puzzled. Before he could get angry again, I explained to him that he needed to apologize to the coop board, not me. I said that before we could turn the no into a yes we had to get the discussion back to rational, rather than emotional, issues. The broker and I explained why the board needed to ask personal questions, comparing it to the questions he would want to ask of anyone who'd be buying a share of his home and living there with him. The broker then telephoned the chairman of the coop board and arranged for him to meet us for a cup of coffee later that evening.

Liam, the broker, and I sat around a table with the chairman, a retired plastic surgeon. Liam didn't wait for us to say anything. He immediately launched into a humble, heartfelt apology, explaining how much pressure he had been under, and admitting that he didn't fully understand the reasons for the board's questions. He politely asked if we could all start over from scratch the next day. The chairman agreed. Liam's offer was accepted two days after that. Liam called me the next week to say that he never thought he'd give his best New York performance in a Starbucks rather than on Broadway.

When I heard Martin Jackson say that he was looking for respect from his company, I knew I couldn't help him over the telephone. It turned out that Martin was going to be in New York City for a couple of hours on an airport layover. I suggested we meet to follow up on our call. We arranged to sit down together at a lounge in JFK International Airport.

Martin did not fit my stereotypical image of a scientist. In fact, he looked more like an investment banker than an engineer or academic. Wearing a dark blue suit with a light blue shirt and yellow tie, and carrying a black leather barrister's case, he emerged from his plane looking no worse for wear after a three-hour flight. Just from his garb and manners I could see how important it was for him to be respected. We sat together in the airport lounge and I explained to him that I thought he was reacting emotionally rather than rationally because he had let the problem fester for so long. With obvious thought he listened carefully to what I had to say. After only a moment's pause he accepted my hypothesis, and asked what he could do. I suggested he spend the next leg of his flight developing a prioritized list of examples of his being disrespected by the corporation. He agreed and said he'd call me when he arrived in Boston later than evening.

When he called, Martin reeled off six or eight examples, all of which dealt with his not having been promoted in grade for the past decade. I asked if he had ever specifically launched a campaign to get a promotion. He admitted he hadn't, adding that he'd never had to do that before. Before I could respond, he himself interjected, "But I guess I need to now." Over the course of the next two weeks Martin and I, working over the telephone, prepared a formal proposal for a promotion. It worked. After ten years of frustration, Martin had finally made it to the next level.

Become an Expert

6

Knowledge is the antidote to fear.

Ralph Waldo Emerson

One of the most vital items in my problem-solving approach is to become an expert. By that I mean, to learn about your own needs and wants, the problem itself, and the needs and wants of any other parties involved.

The obvious importance of knowledge is that it can give you the secret to solving a problem. If you're approaching a banker for a loan you could either fill out the application blindly, or you could first try to become an expert. What are the characteristics of loan applications that the banker has, in the past, accepted and rejected? How can you craft your application so it looks like those successful applications? What are the banker's needs in the process?

Sure, you could wing it, hope for the best, and if you're rejected, work at turning the no into a yes. That's what most people do. Some luck out in the first instance. Others are able to turn a rejection around, either on their own or with my help. However, your odds of success will be much better if you first do your homework. If you find out that in order to get a $25,000 unsecured business line of credit you need to show a profit of at least $100,000 a year for three consecutive years, you've learned the secret to overcoming your problem.

Become an expert on your problems and you'll rarely, if ever, get rejected.

Knowledge has another, less obvious, benefit: it can boost your confidence. Most fear comes from the unknown. When you don't know what an experience, situation, or person is like, your imagination takes over. More often than not, your psyche plays out worst- rather than best-case scenarios. I suppose it's a form of mental self-defense: prepare for the worst. However, it also leads to an almost automatic anxiety and fear of the unknown. You can eliminate this fear by gaining knowledge, by making the unknown, known.

If you're fearful of your meeting with the banker, gather some information about him. What does he look like? Has anyone you're friendly with dealt with him? Does he belong to any civic organizations or clubs? Is he a gourmet cook? In the course of your investigations you may stumble across some essential information. Then again, you may only learn some trivial facts. In either case you'll have helped yourself turn a no into a yes. Anything you learn about the banker will make you feel more secure and poised at your meeting. Even if all you can uncover is a picture of the banker, that will help. Your knowledge of his appearance will let you walk right over to him when you enter the bank. Since you'll already have "met," you'll feel more comfortable and confident when you first shake his hand. And that comfort and confidence will come across, making you a better advocate for your cause.

BECOMING AN EXPERT

There are three ways you can become an expert and, in the process, help overcome your business problems. Each has its advantages and disadvantages.

The first way to become an expert is to receive some formal schooling or training. The advantage of this method of becoming an expert is that it provides you with an official endorsement: you're getting a seal of approval. The disadvantage of pursuing such formal endorsement is that it's time-consuming. In all honesty, such an approach is rarely used by my clients, since it takes such a long time. Most of my clients come to me "in extremis" and therefore can't rely on a long-term educational program to help them turn a no into a yes. The handful of times I've encouraged a client to use this technique have been when I was consulting with a young person, just out of college, who was looking to develop a strategic career plan. For most of my clients, two months, let alone two years, is too long.

The second way to become an expert is through public research. This involves going to the library and looking through books and periodicals, doing searches of online databases, and gathering any other already public information you can. It's truly incredible how much free intelligence you can gather on a specific person or a company simply by consulting the public record. If you're willing to pay for research, say by purchasing a report on a private company or individual from an organization like Dun & Bradstreet, you can obtain even more. The advantages of public research as a method of becoming an expert are that it's quick and relatively easy to do. For the cost of an hour online and an hour of their time anyone who's computer literate can come up with a great deal of information. The disadvantage of this approach is that it's not likely to yield any surprising or unique information. Public research will let you become as much of an expert as anyone else . . . but not more. It's a defensive technique: it insures you won't be surprised. However, it's not going to give you the information to spring any surprises of your own.

The third method of obtaining expertise is to conduct private research. This involves working the telephone and turning your personal network into an information network. Remember, no man (or woman) is an island: there are ways to reach everyone. And bear in mind that, even though it has become a cliché, there really does seem to be only six degrees of separation between any two people. In other words, it may take you at least six telephone calls, but you should be able to get information on anyone by expanding your own network.

Let's say you're looking for information on that banker you're asking for a line of credit. Private research would involve calling your accountant and attorney and asking if they or anyone they knew had any information on the banker. It would include putting out feelers at the chamber of commerce and Kiwanis Club meetings, asking if anyone had relevant information, or if they could steer you to other sources of information. The advantage of private research is that it can provide you with unique and possibly very valuable information. The disadvantage is that it's not easy to do and can be time-consuming. Private research works wonders when it comes to one-on-one negotiations or problems that seem to defy logic. It's an aggressive technique that can provide you with the key to make a personal connection or to solve a stubborn puzzle.

SHOWING YOUR EXPERTISE

Having become an expert, you next must decide whether and how to demonstrate your newly won expertise. First, should you show it at all? Obviously, if demonstrating that you're an expert will help you turn a no into a yes, then make it apparent. If you learn the banker is enamored by the possibilities of the Internet, then clearly it makes sense to bring it up and tell him about your planned Web site. But just as obviously, if exhibiting your expertise will somehow hurt your case—perhaps by intimidating, alienating, or angering the other party—keep your knowledge under wraps. You may have learned that the banker has been married and divorced three times, is a regular on the weekly bus junkets to Vegas, and loves wearing expensive European suits. All that information can give you extra confidence and perhaps an edge in your discussions. That doesn't mean you should ask his advice on dating showgirls.

If you have decided to show your expertise, you next must decide how. If you do it subtly you might succeed in making your point without drawing attention to your public or private research. For instance, the banker, while intrigued by your Web site plan, may not be so enamored of obvious efforts to gather information on him. If you demonstrate your expertise openly you draw attention to your efforts. That might be an added bonus if it reflects well on you or your efforts. The same banker who'd be angered by your personal probing might be quite impressed if you tell him you just finished taking three graduate-level courses in Internet marketing.

Let's look at how some clients of mine became experts and used that expertise to turn no into yes.

VINCE SPINELLI: PRIVATE RESEARCH, NOT DEMONSTRATED

Vince Spinelli has one of the most flexible minds I've ever come into contact with. Lean, olive-skinned and dark-haired, the forty-three-year-old Vince carries himself like a bird of prey: no wasted motion and with a real sense of purpose. Trained in accounting and finance, Vince had worked his way up the ladder of the giant international toy manufacturing firm he had joined right out of grad school. After ten years with the firm, Vince was on track to one day become chief financial officer. However, he viewed that as a dead end. His time with the company had proven to Vince that the only route to the CEO's office—his goal—was through the marketing arm of the company. The board members might be focused on the bottom line—who wasn't these days—but they still saw the financial department as little more than a group of bean counters and the management branch solely as administrators. It was the marketing arm of the company where creativity was rewarded and CEOs were spawned.

Vince, through hard work and creativity, engineered a lateral transfer for himself into marketing. He was an almost instant success. Despite not having any formal training in marketing, Vince was an instinctive salesman. He knew exactly how to simultaneously please both parents and kids. With his financial background, he could couple that instinct with a keen eye on costs. Within two years of the shift he was the prime candidate to become the next vice president of marketing. In the firm, the vice president of marketing was traditionally acknowledged to be second in line to the CEO spot. Currently, however, it was held by an older executive who wasn't likely to ever make it to the throne. Vince's success hadn't gone unnoticed in the industry. He was constantly fielding calls from headhunters looking to fill upper-level management positions at other toy manufacturers. This outside interest came to the attention of the board. As a result, his mentor on the board asked him to sign an employment contract with the company. That's when he came to see me.

Vince's problem was that he had created enemies all over the company. The financial branch saw Vince as a traitor. Those in the marketing division saw Vince as an interloper who had stolen their thunder. By bucking the unwritten rules and procedures of the company he had annoyed the management departments. Vince was smart enough to realize that while the offer of an employment contract was an opportunity, it was also a minefield. After about two hours of discussion, Vince and I decided he needed to become an expert on the internal politics of his company if he was going to succeed. That meant doing some private research.

Vince began by speaking to his mentor on the board, telling her of his fears and asking her for some insight on what the other individual board members thought of him and his climb so far. Simultaneously he called the headhunters whom he had been working with and his contacts in other companies, asking them all for help in getting info on the current head of the marketing department. I tapped into my own network to try to gather information on the attorney who headed up the firm's legal department and who would be the point man in the negotiations.

Vince learned that the majority of the active members of the board thought highly of him and did indeed see him as a future CEO. The three most influential members had entrepreneurial backgrounds and didn't have a problem with his not following a traditional career path. From his headhunter and industry contacts, Vince learned that the current marketing vice president didn't like Vince, since he wasn't one of his own people. But he also learned the current vice president's prime concern was insuring that he survived another two years in the company so he'd be able to retire with his full pension and exercise his stock options. I found out the attorney with whom we'd be negotiating was a young, diligent advocate. He'd be more concerned with the form and structure of the contract than the political maneuvering behind it. He was also, I learned, very eager to make a career for himself in the firm.

Using this information, Vince and I developed a plan. He asked his mentor on the board to have conversations with the three influential board members, asking them to simply let the current head of the marketing department know how highly they valued Vince. His mentor hinted to the marketing vice president that Vince was being seen as a future CEO, and that the board was very eager to keep him. The marketing vice president then went to the head of the legal department and passed along the hint. Once negotiations started, however, Vince and I demonstrated none of the expertise we had gained. There was no need to: calling attention to the outside motives of either the vice president of marketing or the attorney would have done nothing but make them feel uncomfortable. After only a week's worth of discussions Vince signed a lucrative five-year contract.

SANDY VAN PELT: PUBLIC RESEARCH, DEMONSTRATED SUBTLY

I have known Sandy Van Pelt for years. She came to work for me right after graduating from New York University with a bachelor's degree in communications. Sandy was an excellent aide, with terrific interpersonal skills, and a real flair for working with the media people I dealt with when appearing regularly on CNBC television and CBS radio. Her clean-scrubbed, all-American girl looks, and her outgoing personality, made her an exuberant presence in my office. Clients loved her. After two years with me, she left to take a position in the marketing department of a major media company, best known for its family-oriented programming. Sandy's skill and personality served her well there too. She was making a name for herself in New York. So much so that she received a telephone call offering what seemed to be a fabulous job opportunity.

The call came from the owner of a small but very well known television production company. The owner was the widow of the founder of the firm, a much beloved creative genius who unfortunately died quite young. She and her family were continuing the business, and actually doing quite well. Her late husband had successfully institutionalized the creativity that originally came solely from him. A score of talented young people were now continuing his work. The company was using the licensing fees from their early successes as a foundation for new ventures. Sandy had been targeted as just the sort of fresh young person who could fit in with the company. She was offered the spot as director of publicity. Ecstatic, Sandy then telephoned to let me know what was going on and to ask my help in negotiating her salary.

After congratulating her, the first thing I did was get Sandy to slow down. After just a couple of minutes it was clear to me she needed to become much more of an expert on the company that was now pursuing her. Sandy and everyone else knew a great deal about the company's products, it was true. But its inner workings weren't as well known.

Sandy began by going to the New York Public Library's primary business branch and scouring the periodical indexes for mentions of the firm. She spent her next three lunch hours compiling a list of references. At home in the evening she went online and searched the Web for references to the firm. She printed out the results of searches using four different search engines. On Saturday, she went back to the library, pulled the relevant microfiches and bound copies from the stacks, and photocopied them. Returning home, she went back online, downloaded, and then printed the most potentially interesting sites.

On Sunday, rather than spending her day reading the *New York Times*, she dug through all her public research.

I was surprised when my office telephone rang at 7:30 A.M. on Monday. I was doubly surprised when I picked up and heard a glum Sandy. She told me her research had uncovered a problem. The firm that was courting her had been a recent acquisition target of Sandy's current company. The details weren't clear, but apparently the sale was all set to go until the founder suddenly died. At that point the larger corporation, depending on which story you read, either heartlessly backed out of a sealed deal, or wisely decided to renegotiate a still pending sale. Whatever the truth was, there was certainly bad blood between the two firms. That wouldn't have been such a big deal if Sandy hadn't also learned from a recent small item in the financial press that the acquisition talks were still going on, albeit with less fanfare. Sandy and I were both concerned that she could take the new job, earning the enmity of her current company, and then be faced with working for them again if the sale actually went through. It seemed like a recipe for getting dismissed in the near future. We agreed that Sandy would call the owner of the smaller firm and ask for a few more days to think about the offer, and then come to my office later in the day so we could strategize.

After going over Sandy's goals as well as her understandable fears, she and I came up with a plan. She would meet with the president of the small firm, express her excitement about the opportunity, but also state her strong desire for an employment contract. There would be nothing to gain by getting into the details of the battle, so we decided Sandy shouldn't be overt in demonstrating her information. Instead, we decided to present her contract request as a desire to protect herself in case there was a change in ownership that might not be advantageous to her position. This would make it clear that Sandy was astute enough to know of the struggle, but also politic enough not to raise the issue directly. Those traits, added to her already admired skills and abilities, would make her, we thought, an even more attractive candidate.

We were right. Despite her young age and relatively junior level, Sandy was able to negotiate a three-year contract. We both felt that would be long enough for either the deal to fall through, or for her former employer to get over any animosity. Luckily, we were right once again. After two years the acquisition efforts stopped and the outward acrimony came to an end when a quiet, out-of-court settlement was reached.

DAVID ZIMMER: PRIVATE RESEARCH, DEMONSTRATED OPENLY

David Zimmer earned my respect as a skilled adversary. When I met him he was the business manager of a local television channel, responsible for negotiating salary and termination issues with the on-air talent. Since I was an advisor for some of the broadcasters, I sat across the table from him a number of times. A short and wiry forty-year-old, with curly brown hair and a floppy mustache, David was a skilled attorney with a good sense of humor and a ready smile. In such situations, with such a person, it's easy for mutual respect to blossom into friendship. That's why I wasn't surprised when he called to ask my professional advice about his own career.

David confessed that he was bored to tears with being business manager. He had taken the job of business manager five years earlier because he didn't enjoy working in a traditional law firm and thought the entertainment industry would be interesting and lucrative. He was wrong. The work was neither as interesting nor as lucrative as he'd thought. Once he got past the fact that he was negotiating with television stars over larger numbers, the sessions became no more interesting than any other salary discussions. In fact, dealing with those large numbers being batted about with on-air talent and programming people just made his own compensation seem even less adequate than it really was. David had come to me for help in shifting into the management part of the business.*

It clearly wasn't that much of a stretch once you had a chance to hear David speak about television. He clearly knew the business and had some very creative ideas. However, the stumbling block was that he didn't have obvious experience in anything other than the financial end of the business. Convinced that David already had the knowledge

*You've probably noticed that many of my career consultations involve high-level individuals looking to shift careers, businesses, or industries. I think that's due to a couple of factors. First, it's a product of the times we're living in when there are no more career ladders and no more job security. Second, it's a product of the nature of my practice. Most traditional career counselors, whom I have great respect for, tend to focus on the needs of mid-level employees rather than upper-level people.

necessary, I suggested he instead focus on becoming an expert on the culture of his company. He did that through private research. He burned up the telephone expanding and consulting his network, seeking out information on station management in general, and his own station management in specific. After about a week's worth of intense investigation he came across a very valuable tidbit of information.

In speaking with a friend in the home office of the industry's national association, he learned that his station's current general manager, a former union official and state politician, had never graduated college. Like many people who didn't have the chance to earn a higher education, the general manager had an almost religious admiration for academia and learning. That became the key to our strategy.

David launched a campaign to teach a course in cable television at a local college. He spent weeks developing a syllabus and reading list that he then worked into a very impressive proposal. David received two requests to teach the class in the next semester. Knowing that we would need to raise David's profile in order to move into an expanded role, we decided to openly make use of his information.

With the two class commitments and a copy of his syllabus in hand, David asked to meet with the station manager. Explaining that he'd heard of the station manager's strong commitment to higher education, David asked his boss if he'd be willing to come to his classes to serve as a guest lecturer. His boss was overjoyed at the prospect and quite impressed by the syllabus.

Next, David enlisted the help of a freelance writer to turn his course syllabus into a book proposal. David shopped the proposal around to textbook publishers and after only a couple of rejections, was able to land a deal. Of course, he quickly brought the news to the station manager in the guise of a request for his boss to contribute a chapter.

The third-party endorsements of his expertise from two colleges and a publisher were enough to make David a prime candidate for the assistant general manager's position when it opened up the next year. He got the job.

Expertise is extraordinarily powerful in turning no into yes. But there's something even more powerful: trust.

Create an Environment of Trust 7

You know what charm is: a way of getting the answer yes without having asked any clear question.

Albert Camus, The Fall

You can receive no greater gift than someone's trust. In business, when you're trusted by someone else it means they believe you will place their needs and interests on a par with your own. It's trust that allows two businesspeople to work out a deal that's mutually beneficial, each getting all they need, if not all they want. And it's trust that lets someone go out on a limb, break a rule, or accept a loss of face, by reversing course or bucking a trend. Remember, in business, no is the automatic, almost instinctive response to any situation, since it reinforces the status quo. No one gets fired for saying no. When the person you're dealing with trusts you, however, it's much easier to turn a no into a yes.

That's great for those who deal with the same individuals over and over again. When two parties have a long history of mutual respect and cooperation, trust is the natural result. Time is to trust what good soil is to plants. So, it's relatively easy to turn a no from your spouse, a family member, or a friend into a yes. They've known you for a long time and you've a history together.

But unfortunately, many, if not most, of today's business and financial dealings are between two people with little or no history. Generally, the banker you're approaching for an operating capital loan won't know you or your business and, in fact, won't be staying at that branch long enough to get to know you or your business. The supervisor you're asking for a raise may have only come on board a year ago, or it could be you who just recently joined the team. In today's business world people move too quickly for trust to develop naturally. Personally, I think that's why there's an ever increasing trend toward quantifying every business relationship and deal entirely with numbers and memorializing all of them with formal contracts. You can't (and probably shouldn't) accept the word or handshake of someone you've never met before. I also think that's why there are more nos that need to be turned into yeses today than ever before.

Since trust is an essential ingredient in solving problems, and since you can no longer count on it developing naturally in our fast-paced business world, it needs to be intentionally cultivated . . . quickly. I've been facing this hurdle ever since I became a legal consultant. In order for me to provide quality service to my clients, I need them to open up to me and feel comfortable enough to discuss what may be very painful, personal issues. That, obviously, requires them to trust me.

I must admit I've always had a skill for gaining people's trust. I think I inherited it from my father, who has always been able to connect with people very quickly. Before I went into private practice, my instinctive abilities at gaining trust were enough to get me through the common business situations I faced. But when I launched my consulting business I knew I'd need to do better. That led me to do an informal study of how to develop trust. I spoke with businesspeople I admired and . . . trusted. I read everything on the subject I could get my hands on, from Benjamin Franklin to Norman Vincent Peale. I tried out techniques on family and friends. Finally, I used the techniques on my earliest clients, refining the devices that worked and discarding those that didn't. All this research, trial and error, and refinement allowed me to develop a system for creating trust within twenty-four hours of meeting someone.

THE SHORTCUT TO TRUST

The keystone of my technique is a simple but very powerful truth: the shortcut to trust is caring.

One of the feelings that develops over time and which naturally leads to trust is the sense that the other person cares for you and your well-being. That means more than having shared interests or similar beliefs. Caring represents a personal connection that transcends the reasons or circumstances that brought the two of you together. Caring is perceived as an emotional bond that goes far deeper than a shared mercenary interest.

Normally, the feeling that someone cares about you builds slowly and incrementally through small and subtle acts and statements. These might include gestures like bringing you a cup of coffee, coming outside of a private office to greet you at the door, or asking about your family with obvious interest. Over weeks and months such little actions lead to a sense of caring and translate into a feeling of trust. The trusting relationship is like a giant fortress that's actually built from little pebbles of caring behaviors.

My technique involves using as many of these caring behaviors, both subtle and obvious, as I possibly can, as quickly as possible. In effect, I overwhelm the other person with signs that I care for them as a human being. That allows them to trust me within twenty-four hours of meeting me. I make sure people who call for appointments are treated well. I insist my staff greet clients warmly when they arrive at my office, taking their coats, offering them coffee, tea, or water, asking if they'd like to use the rest room or telephone, and showing them to a comfortable chair. I always come out of my office to greet clients. I smile and introduce myself, using their name as well as my own, and express my gratitude for their coming. I repeat all the offers earlier made by my staff, making doubly sure they were extended. I openly tell my staff not to disturb me with calls unless they're emergencies. I personally escort the clients into my office where we sit around a table. During the course of the consultation I ask about the client's physical as well as their business or financial health, and their home as well as their work environment. At first, I listen more than I talk, leaning forward in my chair and looking them in the eye when they speak. After we discuss their problem, I give them something from my office to take home, whether it's the pad they borrowed to take notes, or a book they might find useful or interesting. I once again escort them out of my office and repeat all the offers made when they first arrived. I thank them for coming into my life and shake hands with greater intimacy and warmth than when they arrived, this time using both hands. Then, later that day, either I or someone from my office follows up over the telephone, asking if they had any questions or needed anything else prior to their next visit.

Spelled out this way, my techniques sound very obvious. That's because they are. But what's also conspicuous is that they're for real. Sure they're conscious, but that doesn't make them any less heartfelt. I do care about my clients. I am concerned with their physical well-being and comfort. I want them to feel welcome and at ease in my office. All I'm doing is demonstrating what I feel and think through my words and deeds. I'm wearing my heart on my sleeve and letting them see it. My technique is no more mercenary than saying "please," "thank you," or "you're welcome."

Is my system manipulative on some level? I suppose so. But I don't believe that makes it bad or wrong. I'm not using it to twist people's arms into buying something worthless, or con them out of their life savings. I'm simply trying to quickly create sufficient intimacy for me to be able to help them overcome their problems. I'm not using these techniques to pull unsuspecting people into my office. I'm using these techniques to assist those who have come in on their own, looking for my help. And then, I'm teaching the same techniques to all my clients and readers. I guess I'm saying the ends and my motivation justify my means, and that the ends you're pursuing and your motivations should also justify the means.

If being openly warm and caring can today be construed by many people as Machiavellian then it says more about our current business environment than it does about my techniques. And if everyone practices the technique I espouse what will happen? We will all be more civil, polite, and kind to one another while overcoming most of our problems.

My technique for demonstrating caring and generating trust consists of nine elements:

- facial expressions
- body language
- garb
- personal space and physical comfort
- asking questions and listening

- choice of words and language
- demonstrating and expressing gratitude
- showing humility, and
- exceeding expectations.

Let's look at each of the nine, both in theory and in practice.

FACIAL EXPRESSIONS

Most facial expressions are instinctive rather than conscious. Because of that, many of us have learned to suppress our facial expressions in business settings and to instead convey what we think is a neutral countenance. We don't want to "give away" our feelings. However, I don't think there is such a thing as a neutral countenance. A blank expression isn't perceived as neutral, it's perceived as coldness, disinterest, or worse yet, stupidity.

If you want to demonstrate that you care, simply stop suppressing facial expressions. When you're told something serious, you'll appear concerned. When you're told something tragic, you'll appear sad. And when you're told something happy, you'll smile. Smiles are contagious. They are also one of the clearest signals you can give to another human being that you're interested in them and consider them important. It may sound crazy, but you really can turn your business or career around simply by smiling more, and that's what happened to Janet Parsons.

An on-air radio personality, Janet came to me for help after being given a negative performance review by the station manager. What was odd was that the negative elements had little to do with her actual performance. Her ratings were good and she came across very well on the air. What the station manager dwelt on, however, was her attitude. When prodded for specific examples, he couldn't offer any. It was, he said, a feeling he had: she "looked unhappy." When she told me the story I could see the problem. Janet's mouth naturally turned down at the corners, making even a blank expression look like a frown. It shouldn't have had anything to do with her review, and clearly the station manager would have never brought up such an issue with a male employee, but despite the unfairness of the situation, it had to be dealt with.

The solution was simple. While continuing to actively promote her positive performance, Janet began smiling broadly whenever she wasn't in her private office. She asked a friend on the staff to give her a sign (tugging an earlobe) if she ever let the grin slip. Janet kept that smile plastered on her face when she walked down the hall and when she sat in meetings. Six months later, after changing nothing other than the expression on her face, she went in for another review. The positive change in her attitude, according to the station manager, was nothing less than astounding.

BODY LANGUAGE

Body language, like facial expression, is instinctive. However, for some reason, it is easier to consciously control. Unfortunately, most people don't take full advantage of that control. Few of us need to be told to sit up straight rather than slouch in a chair during a business meeting, to not touch our faces, to look at someone when they're speaking, or to keep from crossing our arms across our chests. Those are all defensive maneuvers, designed to keep from creating negative perceptions. In order to show that you care about another person you need to go one step further and create positive perceptions. I suggest doing this through the angle of your upper body when seated and the way you say good-bye.

When you're sitting down in a meeting pay attention to the distance between your upper body and the other party. When they're speaking, don't just make eye contact, lean a bit forward as well. This demonstrates rapt interest and extreme attention. When it's time for you to answer a question, break eye contact momentarily and lean slightly backward. This conveys deep thought. Then, when it's time for you to deliver a message to the other party, reestablish eye contact and lean forward once again, displaying your concern and conviction.

When you first meet someone, a firm handshake is expected. But at the conclusion of the meeting take it one step further . . . or one hand further. When I'm saying good-bye to a male client I look him in the eye, shake his hand with my right hand, and put my left hand either on his forearm or his right shoulder. When I'm saying good-bye to a female client I also make eye contact, and shake her right hand, but in this instance I bow slightly from the waist and put my left hand on top of our two shaking right hands. This slight variation from the initial greeting conveys gratitude and solidifies the new level of intimacy we've achieved.

Bill Schneider's problem wasn't solidifying intimacy, it was inspiring confidence: an unusual problem for someone six foot eight and over three hundred pounds. I had gotten to know Bill when he was a successful advertising space salesman for a weekly news magazine: he worked on some special small business sections I had helped prepare. Bill had come up through the ranks and had spent the past fifteen years selling to the same group of customers. His clients had come up through the ranks along with him. They all knew and liked one another. In that kind of environment Bill's soft-spoken, mild manner played very well. In fact, it contributed to his persona as a "gentle giant." Unfortunately, this gentle giant was laid off during a round of corporate downsizing. After a year of being unable to find another job Bill called me.

Bill's experience and résumé had won him many interviews over the past twelve months, but every one had resulted in a no. He wanted to see me to learn how to turn those nos into at least one yes. I told him to arrive at my office for his appointment as if he were meeting me for a job interview. From the moment I went out to greet him his problem was obvious. Due to his height, Bill had a habit of slouching. And because of his sheer physical size he went out of his way to shake hands very gently. Once you knew him, these traits were endearing. At first, however, they were off-putting. His size accentuated the limpness of his handshake. Couple that with his slouch and he seemed totally lacking in confidence: the last thing you'd want in a salesperson. I told Bill what I thought and encouraged him to use his size rather than be embarrassed by it, to physically dominate the room when he entered it. All we did for the rest of his appointment was block out his actions and movements for future interviews. Bill's first interview after our meeting landed him a new position.

GARB AND HYGIENE

Every businessperson knows that in order to make a good impression, he or she must be well dressed and groomed. The same is true if you want to show you care and develop trust. Generally, this is a defensive approach. Your appearance must at least match what the other party expects. If you don't look the part, you're signaling, intentionally or not, that you don't care about industry norms. Iconoclasts may be interesting, but they don't inspire trust. Of course, the specifics of your appearance depend on your industry and situation. A legal or financial professional or a corporate executive needs to be cloaked in a conservative business suit. A midlevel sales or marketing person or a creative professional can be a bit less staid. A younger sales or marketing person or creative individual is expected to be trendy. The key is to meet expectations. Show up in a three-piece suit for an interview to land a computer graphics assignment and you'll raise eyebrows as high as if you showed up to meet a legal client wearing a pair of Dr. Martens.

There's only one instance that I can recall of garb and hygiene actually being used as more than just a defensive measure. Andrew Douglas came to me for help in formulating a promotion request. A structural engineer working for a new automaker, Andrew had been stuck at the same career level for five years. Together we formulated a good plan and then prepared a powerful memo outlining Andrew's case. Andrew was supremely confident . . . until he made his appointment to speak with his supervisor. Andrew called me in a tizzy. I asked what was wrong and he said that his meeting was set for Friday morning. I said I didn't understand the problem. He explained that Fridays were dress-down days. Andrew felt like he was facing a catch-22. Dress formally, as he normally would for a business meeting of this importance, and he'd stick out like a sore thumb. Dress informally and his request might not be taken as seriously. After I calmed him down we came up with a solution. Andrew dressed formally but used his out-of-the-norm garb as an icebreaker at the meeting. He started by saying that even though it was a dress-down day he wanted to dress in a manner that reflected his respect and admiration for his superior and the company. At that point, his boss literally rose from his chair, shook Andrew's hand, and thanked him. The promotion was clinched right then.

PERSONAL SPACE AND PHYSICAL COMFORT

The more comfortable a person is, psychologically and physically, the more relaxed he'll be and the more ready he'll be to trust someone else. Showing that you care about a person's psychological and physical comfort does as much as actually contributing to their comfort. This is one instance where it really is the thought that counts. For instance, you are never going to be able to make someone who comes to your office feel totally at home. However, by making the effort, you do enough to get them to trust you. Your efforts to make other people comfortable may go further than just asking if they want something to drink or if they'd like to use the bathroom. Take the case of Ronnie Taylor.

Ronnie was the thirty-seven-year-old son of one of my Connecticut neighbors.* He had just taken over the accounting department of a small manufacturing company located in New York's Hudson Valley. Ronnie had spent ten years at a "big five" accounting firm prior to joining the company. He had been recruited by a schoolmate, whose family were the majority shareholders of the business. The plan was for Ronnie to take over the financial operations of the firm within two years, when his friend was scheduled to take over management. The problem was their plan didn't take into account the chairman, his friend's seventy-eight-year-old father.

The older man was willing but not eager to hand over the management reins to his son. However, he was digging in his heels about turning over the purse strings to Ronnie. The more Ronnie told me about the older man, the more it was clear he was deeply proud of his business. Still, his health was failing. He had lost hearing in one ear and was having trouble seeing. But because he was so proud, everyone in the company pretended not to notice. Ronnie and I decided that could be our opportunity. Starting the next week, Ronnie printed out the weekly reports in a larger typeface. When they met together, Ronnie made sure to stand or sit on the side of the older man's good ear. However, he never said anything about it, nor called any attention to his actions . . . he just started doing them. After three months the older man had taken to calling Ronnie his "adopted son" and had become the primary advocate of his taking over as chief financial officer.

ASKING QUESTIONS AND LISTENING—BEING CURIOUS

The highest compliment you can pay to a new business acquaintance is to ask questions about something he or she is interested in, and then listen intently to his or her answers. The effect never fails to be amaz-

---

*My wife and I spend most of our weekends at our farmhouse in Connecticut.

ing. This technique on its own is often enough to generate an almost instantaneous personal warmth.

I saw this most clearly at one of my family's Thanksgiving dinners. My son Michael asked if he could bring a friend to dinner: a young writer named Mitchell Bronstein. We set another place at the table, never thinking that by the end of dinner, Mitchell would be the star of the evening. An unassuming, and to be honest, plain-looking young man of thirty, Mitchell was polite and, at first, shy. But after being introduced to everyone, he began winning us all over, one by one. It was only in retrospect that I figured out how he did it. Rather than fading into the background, or concentrating his attention on my son, whom he already knew, Mitchell made a point of speaking with each of us. Instead of just making small talk, he asked everyone about themselves. And then, rather than just nodding, he actually listened . . . carefully . . . and then followed up with further questions. As I said, by the end of the evening, he was my family's favorite person.

Since that Thanksgiving dinner I've used the same technique myself and suggested it to many of my clients. It works particularly well when you're meeting someone who isn't a trained professional interviewer, for example, if you're on a job interview with an executive of a company, rather than with a human resources person, or if you're negotiating a contract with a manager, rather than an attorney. The questions needn't even be about business per se. If you see your opposite number is, let's say, a photographer, you could ask her about the shots adorning her office wall. All that matters is you ask questions that show respect for her knowledge, and then listen carefully to her answers.

CHOICE OF WORDS AND LANGUAGE

I'm sure you've heard the cliché that sometimes it's not what you say, but how you say it. This is one cliché that's accurate. Slang, curses, and even some colloquial expressions are obviously out of bounds in business situations. But just as important are the careful selection of pronouns, the use of words that demonstrate respect, and making an effort to use the other party's language.

Whenever you're conveying negative information use the pronoun "I"; and when you're delivering positive information use the pronoun "we." Most people instinctively look to pass the buck, at least verbally, when giving bad news. Similarly, they reflexively look to take credit when presenting good news. This has the opposite effect from what's intended. Rather than insulating you from blame or gaining you more credit, it usually serves to paint you as self-serving. To be able to turn a no into yes you need to at least seem to be putting the other party's interests above your own. That means you should verbally accept responsibility, if not blame, for negative events, and be eager to share or even give away credit for successes. Most people in business aren't foolish: they'll know whether or not you're to blame or deserve credit for something. Ironically, by appearing to act counter to your own interests you actually do more for yourself by gaining the trust of the other party. Readily accept responsibility for screwups and you'll end up bearing less blame. Eagerly pass along credit for successes and you'll actually accrue more kudos.

Even though you're trying to establish some level of caring intimacy with others in an effort to establish trust, you should use the most respectful language possible until told otherwise. Calling someone by their first name without being asked to do so may be common practice today. But that doesn't mean it will help you turn no into yes. Such an automatic assumption of intimacy will usually backfire. It's presumptuous, and in some cases even demeaning. Personally, I'm not comfortable having someone young enough to be my daughter call me "Steve." I can only imagine how annoying it must be for an older woman to have some young man call her by her first name. Is this a generational problem? Perhaps. But nevertheless, I think calling someone Mr. or Ms. until told otherwise is a traditional sign of respect that's more effective nowadays because it's so rare.

Finally, I suggest that if you're doing business with people whose first language isn't English, you should try to master at least one or two relevant words or phrases in the client's language. Trying to converse at length in a language in which you're not fluent is a mistake. Not only will you have problems making yourself understood, but you're also apt to offend. At the same time, making no effort to communicate in the other person's language is a sign of disrespect.

Jack Goldblatt came to see me just prior to a two-month project in Germany. Jack's assignment was to help establish the new German advertising sales division of a cable television channel that was about to go international. I represent some other executives at the channel where he worked, and they suggested he come see me for help in solving his problem, since they knew I worked for quite a few foreign clients. Jack's initial telephone conversations with his German contacts had not gone well. He had been told they all spoke English fluently, yet he felt there was a communication gap. The more he described his conversations, it became obvious that it was his aggressive, almost arrogant manner and language that might not be going over very well with salespeople who were already feeling anxious. I suggested he pick up a phrase book and try to add a few German words to his conversations. After just a couple of calls in which he tossed off words like *musikalisch* and *Fernsehapparat*, and phrases like *ins Kino gehen* he had broken the ice with his German contacts. Showing that he respected them enough to pick up a few words and phrases enabled him to gain their trust and overcome his problem.

DEMONSTRATING AND EXPRESSING GRATITUDE

Thank you is an incredibly powerful phrase regardless of the language in which it is spoken. That's why I tell my clients to use it as often as possible to go beyond just words in demonstrating their gratitude.

Expressions of gratitude at the successful conclusion of a transaction are expected, and therefore they are only really noted when absent. Thanks offered at the beginning of meetings, or in the midst of negotiations, have more impact because of their rarity. *Begin* discussions with your superiors or customers by thanking them for their past and present guidance or support. During a dialogue, if the other party makes a significant concession or comes up with an insightful idea, immediately express thanks right then and there. Of course, meetings and discussions should close with the obligatory thanks as well.

Be on the alert for any nonverbal gesture you could make to express your gratitude. Let's say you discover the other person is a lover of crossword puzzles. After a meeting you could arrange for them to receive a subscription to the *New York Times* crossword puzzle service.* In order to insure such demonstrations of gratitude aren't misconstrued as bribes, it's important they both involve some personal interest you've learned about in conversation, rather than business, and that

---

*By the way, there actually is such a service. It regularly sends subscribers classic puzzles from the newspaper's past as well as new, unpublished puzzles.

they're not too expensive. You don't want to put someone in the position of owing you too much. Their ego will suffer. If they feel obligated by an excessive show of gratitude they'll end up resenting you.

Debbie Jablonowski had come to me for help in shifting her career from acting to writing. I'd helped her work out a plan, as well as build up a network of contacts. Already skilled in interpersonal communications, Debbie became a master at creating trust in her networking meetings. That was especially important in her case, since writers are often reticent about sharing their contacts. Debbie would begin every meeting by thanking the other person (usually a writer) for taking the time out to see her. She would express thanks for every insight or bit of advice offered during the conversation. Of course, she'd offer her thanks at the close of the meeting, but she didn't leave it there. Since it was common in these meetings for the subject of favorite books and authors to come up, Debbie would always make a note of the other person's interests. As soon as she got home she'd arrange to have a book dealing with the other person's interest sent to them as a gift. It never cost her more than twenty dollars, and yet by the end of three months she had a network of established writers who were actively helping her launch her own career.

SHOWING HUMILITY

Pretense and pomposity raise everyone's hackles. Conversely, unaffected modesty is the most universally endearing trait. Yet being humble runs contrary to popular wisdom, which says that if you don't blow your own horn no one else will. I believe there is a middle ground, which actually gives you the best chance to turn no into yes.

Being humble doesn't mean denigrating your skills or achievements, and it doesn't require you to keep others from blowing your horn. Don't be a blatant self-promoter, but at the same time, don't refuse credit when it's due. When someone compliments you on a job well done, express your gratitude for their words. Never say, "It was nothing." Instead say something like "that's what you pay me to do," or "I'm just earning my fee." Then, ask the satisfied client, customer, or superior to spread the word about your skills and abilities, noting that it would especially mean a lot coming from someone as respected as them.

You can also demonstrate personal humility, which will carry over into your business reputation, by asking for personal help or favors. Most people enjoy granting minor requests, especially if they involve a personal interest of theirs. By asking for a small favor you put yourself in the position of supplicant and the other person in the role of benefactor. By giving them a chance to do something they like, and then get thanked for it, you'll have boosted their ego and their trust in you.

This technique worked wonders for Paula Tanzeri. Paula had come to me for help in negotiating an employment contract. An upper-level executive at a major international auction house, Paula was in the unenviable position of having to negotiate directly with her immediate superior, since he was the only one with the power to make these kinds of decisions. After four days of back and forth discussions, Paula and I could tell the tenor of the meetings was about to turn for the worse over the weekend. In an effort to show some humility without backing down on any of her business demands, Paula sent her boss a personal note, asking if she could borrow a pair of antique candlesticks he cherished for a dinner she was making that coming Friday for her future in-laws. He immediately called Paula and said he'd be happy to lend them to her. On Monday morning she sent him another personal note, expressing her heartfelt thanks. That afternoon's negotiating session was friendlier and more productive than any held the previous week. By Tuesday afternoon her contract was signed and sealed.

EXCEEDING EXPECTATIONS

In today's curt and competitive business world, hard work and excellent service are expected. Arriving early and leaving late won't set you apart. Neither will being attentive to a client's or customer's needs. While these traits will indeed help you *keep* your job and customers, they won't help you move up or expand your business. To do that you need to exceed today's high expectations.

I know: you're already working sixty hours a week and treating your clients like royalty, so you're wondering what more you could do. I suggest you focus, not on trying to redouble your already superhuman initial efforts, but on improving your follow-up. Because everyone today is working so hard on providing initial quality and service, there has been a falloff in follow-up. So much time and effort is going toward actually doing the work in the first place that there's no time for second efforts. That provides you with an opportunity to show how much more caring you are than everyone else, and as a result, how much more deserving you are of trust.

After you've provided your service or done your job, check to see if there are any further questions or needs. This can be done with a telephone call or even an E-mail message. Follow up to see if, for instance, your report arrived on time, and after checking on delivery, ask if it raised any new issues. After selling a product, check back a week later to see how the customer likes their purchase, and to find out if they have any questions. If finding the time for such efforts is a problem, consider making it a part of your evening or weekend schedule. Actually getting to speak with the other person isn't as important in this instance as demonstrating that you're willing to go the extra mile. Leaving a message on an after-hours answering machine or sending a weekend E-mail that's not read until Monday will serve just as well as a Wednesday afternoon telephone conversation.

That's how Jeremy Tarquette managed it. A thirty-four-year-old tax and small business accountant, Jeremy came to me for help in building up his fledgling practice. He had been able to bring a core of clients along with him to his new business two years ago, when he left the medium-size suburban firm he'd joined fresh out of college. But he hadn't been able to expand that client list. Even though he asked all his existing clients to refer him to others, it didn't seem to be working. After we analyzed his business and his techniques, Jeremy and I realized that, while he was good at what he did and provided excellent service, so did dozens of other sole practitioners in his area. Every CPA worth his calculator was sending out newsletters and speaking at Lions Club luncheons. Jeremy needed to do something to set himself apart. He decided to devote one hour every Saturday morning to follow-up. If he and a client usually communicated by E-mail, Jeremy would dash off a quick weekly follow-up note and send it along. If he and a client usually spoke on the telephone, he'd leave a short voice mail message, saying that he was just calling to check in and see if there were any problems. The messages actually generated very little direct feedback. After all, if clients had problems they would have called. Still, that wasn't his intent. It took about four months, but Jeremy began to notice an increase in the number of referrals he was getting. When he asked the new clients what led them to his office, the rely was almost always some variation of: "I heard that you really cared about you clients." As a result, Jeremy was now someone special; someone deserving of trust.

Turn No into Yes

8

"Yes," I answered you last night;
"No," this morning, sir, I say:
Colors seen by candlelight
Will not look the same by day.
Elizabeth Barrett Browning, "The Lady's 'Yes'"

I'm the first to admit there will be times when, despite all your efforts at analyzing problems, developing expertise, and creating trust, you'll still be faced with a no. But that doesn't mean you've failed. You can still overcome that obstacle if you accept that, outside of courtrooms, no is rarely a carefully reasoned judgment. Generally, no is either a quick reaction to a set of sketchy facts, or a reflexive response based on emotions or intuition.

When someone says yes they're electing to make a change, whether it's to increase your salary or to buy your product or service. Saying no means sticking with the status quo. Regardless of how unsatisfactory the current state may be, it's at least a known quantity. The status quo might be bad, but, because it's known, it's not frightening. Many a manager keeps from firing a poor employee because she thinks the replacement could be worse. A potential client or customer fails to hire a new professional or vendor because he would rather stick with "the devil he knows."

Even the savviest businesspeople who aren't afraid of change usually come to a quick unreasoned no. That's because they understand it is far more difficult to turn a yes into a no, than a no into a yes. Having agreed to change the status quo by saying yes, it's nearly impossible to turn back the clock. On the other hand, having maintained the status quo by saying no, it's still possible to rethink the matter, say yes, and elect to change. These people already know that once you learn how, it's relatively easy to turn no into yes.

THE TWO NOS

I divide all outright rejections into two categories: reactions to facts or emotional decisions.

The potential client who decides against hiring you because she thinks your fee is too high is reacting to the set of facts she has been provided. You've told her what you've done for others, what you could do for her, and how much it will cost her. She has decided that, based on the facts you've provided, she isn't willing to spend the money now for what you're willing to do now.

The potential employer who decides against hiring you because he doesn't like your Mississippi accent is making an emotional decision. He has decided that, because he hated the southerner he once worked for, he hates all southerners.

Both reactions to facts and emotional decisions can be turned around, ironically, in the same manner. All you need to do is find out what was behind the no, and then ask for a reconsideration based on new facts.

WHAT'S BEHIND THE NO?

To turn any rejection around you first need to uncover what led to the no. In a few instances, such as rejections from lending institutions, the law requires that you be given a specific reason. In most other cases you can find out what was behind the no simply by asking.

If you're turned down for a raise, ask your superior why. If a customer won't buy your product, ask her why. Frame the question as a search for self-improvement, not as an accusation. Don't even hint at any efforts to turn the no around. Say that you'd be eternally grateful, and that it would be of terrific help in your future efforts, if they would tell you why they chose not to give you a raise, hire you, or buy your product. People who have reacted to facts presented will, after sensing your acceptance of their reaction, meet such a humble request by readily telling you the truth. Remember how effective humility was in establishing trust? Well, it's just as powerful in ferreting out what is behind the no. Having turned you down once already they'll be eager to readily comply with your request, if for no other reason than it will help assuage their guilt.

Even people who have responded with an emotional no, will, when prompted in this modest manner, give you a reason for their rejection. Of course, they probably won't tell you the truth. It would be too embarrassing, or self-incriminating for someone to reveal the emotional basis behind a no. On some level, they know they're being unjust (ethically or legally) in deciding a business issue emotionally. When prompted for a reason they will be forced to cover up their injustice by offering some factual reason. In effect, by asking for a reason you turn their emotional decision into a reaction to facts. Once they give you a factual reason for their no, they can never safely backtrack and claim it was an emotional decision. All they can do is keep coming up with other factual reasons. And no matter how many reasons they continue to come up with you've succeeded in turning their emotional no into a rational no.

By humbly asking why someone said no you'll be given a reason. When you're given a reason, or even multiple reasons, for the rejection, you've also been handed the key for turning it into an acceptance.

RECONSIDERATION BASED ON NEW FACTS

The way to turn a no into a yes is to address the reason for the no. Be careful. I wrote *address*, not *attack*. If you *attack* the other party's honesty, logic, judgment, intelligence, understanding, or analysis you will turn that "no" into a "no way in hell," rather than a yes. Implying or suggesting the other party has made a mistake will only force him to dig in his heels to defend his position and insure he doesn't lose face. Asking someone to change her mind is the equivalent of pouring concrete around her feet: she will never change her position.

Instead of asking for a change of mind, you need to ask for a reconsideration, based on new facts, facts that just happen to address the very points cited as being behind the no. Blame *yourself* for not having understood the situation in the first place. Say *you* made a terrible error in failing to include certain information. Explain that *you* forgot to provide all the necessary information.

Americans revere justice and the appeals process. We love the notion that last-minute revelations of new information can keep an injustice from being committed. It's so ingrained that it has become a recurrent motif in American literature, television, and film. Most people will be happy to play a part in such an exculpatory adventure. If you come to someone as a supplicant, offering new information, he will almost certainly agree to listen and see if the new facts could change his reaction.

And if the decision was actually originally based on emotion, rather than facts, he will be under tremendous emotional pressure to now make an objective decision. Having been forced to give a factual reason for his emotional decision, and then having been offered new exculpatory facts, it will be very hard for him to say no again. Being provided with new facts also makes available a face-saving way of reversing one's emotion-based decision. But even if he does say no, he will now be forced to provide yet another factual reason, which can, of course, be appealed with new facts. Repeated emotional nos cloaked in fake objections can only go on so long before the charade becomes apparent . . . and legally actionable.*

COMING UP WITH NEW FACTS

Where do you come up with new facts? To use one of today's catch-phrases, you need to think "outside the box."

Let's say you learn you were turned down for a line of credit for your business because your loan application didn't show sufficient annual revenue for the size of the credit line. You could submit a new application that included accounts receivable you had previously allocated to January of next year in an effort to defer income. You could also include financial statements for the past five years, and projections for

---

*Of course, there's another issue involved here. Do you really want to work for, or with, someone who is so irrationally biased against you? Is it worth it to force, let's say, a bigot to turn his no into a yes? I don't think there's any ironclad answer; it depends on the situation. While you probably wouldn't want to work as an employee for such an individual, getting him to buy your company's products might be okay.

the next two years, which demonstrate that this year's lower figures are just an ill-timed aberration. You could include additional sources of income—perhaps from part-time consulting work—that you had forgotten to include in your original application. And, of course, you could demonstrate that your needs have changed so you don't need as large a credit line as you originally anticipated.

Perhaps a client decides not to hire you because your fee is too high. You could suggest passing more of the work on to your lower-priced staff. You could offer to divide the job into segments and only take on part of the project, with the client doing the rest in house. You could offer to accept partial payment in advance, while offering to defer final payment until the project is completed.

The new facts you offer are limited only by your ingenuity and creativity. I'll offer a number of relevant scenarios for use in common business situations in the latter parts of this book. But for now, let me tell you the stories of two clients and how they used more unusual methods to successfully turn no into yes.

FRED PINTER SHOWS HE CARES

For Fred Pinter it was love at first sight. The moment he walked into the converted warehouse building and saw the view from the enormous lobby he was hooked. Then when he saw the apartment itself the deal was cinched. The spacious, light, three-bedroom unit on an upper floor, with a view of the Manhattan skyline, was the apartment of his dreams. Sometimes, however, dreams can turn into nightmares.

Fred, a twenty-nine-year-old bachelor, was able to buy the coop apartment for a very good price (for New York City), since it was located in a questionable neighborhood: a formerly industrial section of the Brooklyn waterfront. The area primarily consisted of abandoned factories and warehouses. The few commercial sites in the vicinity were check cashing shops and rundown bars. It was a long walk to the nearest subway stop, and bus service was thin. Still, Fred was ecstatic when he first moved in. Two months earlier he had left the management consulting firm he had been with since grad school for a marketing job with one of the city's hottest Internet companies. He saw his buying the apartment as being parallel to his taking the new job: getting in on the ground floor of an impending boom. Fred felt like he was a pioneer, staking his claim. He didn't know he'd have to pull up stakes so soon.

Fred's new company began taking over more and more of the niche Internet market it had helped create. In the few spare moments Fred and his coworkers had to shoot the breeze, the main topic of conversation was how they were all going to spend their windfalls when the firm went public. Then, one Saturday when he was jogging over the Brooklyn Bridge to the office, he heard a troubling report on the radio. There was a rumor that his company was about to be bought up by a large, already well-established Internet firm in the Northwest. Fred knew that Internet rumors came and went daily, but he also knew that where there was smoke, there was usually fire. He spent a nervous weekend wondering what Monday would bring. What it did bring was a plane ticket.

Fred and all the other upper-level executives of the company found first-class round-trip tickets to Seattle on their desks Monday morning. At a breakfast meeting that morning the two founders of the firm confirmed that the company was indeed being acquired. The good news was that everyone's job was safe. The bad news was that those jobs would be located in Seattle. There was no question in Fred's mind about what he'd do: he was moving with the company. The career and financial opportunities the move presented were just too good to pass up. He immediately contacted a real estate broker and put his apartment up for sale. That was when his problems began.

Where Fred and his fellow coop owners had seen long-term potential, most other people saw urban decay. Not only didn't he get any offers, but only two potential buyers even bothered to look at the place . . . and one of those wouldn't even enter the building. With only a month left before his move, Fred sat down with the coop board and asked for permission to rent his apartment. He thought it was just a formality and was shocked three days later when he received written notice that his request had been turned down. That's when, at the advice of his real estate broker, he came to see me. Together, Fred and I began to look for what was behind the no.

The formal reason given for the rejection was simply that it was against the coop's policy. Since Fred wasn't friendly with any of the other residents he didn't have anyone he could turn to for further information. My office made some discreet inquiries, but they weren't successful. We turned to the broker for help. Since she and I worked together quite often, and she still wished to be able to sell Fred's apartment someday, we had some leverage with her. She was able to talk to her contacts in the building, one of whom sat on the board, and come to us a week later with the inside story.

It turned out that the board wasn't viewing Fred as someone in desperate straits. Instead, they thought he was a speculator, looking to hold on to the apartment as an investment. Most of the other residents were not as affluent as Fred. Many worked in theater and music and had stretched to make what, for Fred, was an inexpensive purchase. They wanted to create a community and were dead set against both absentee ownership and renting. It was clear to us that Fred hadn't provided sufficient facts to show that he financially needed to either sell or rent. Perhaps just as importantly, Fred hadn't demonstrated that he was as committed to the community as anyone else—he just happened to be forced into a move.

Fred asked to speak at the next board meeting. He made it clear that he wasn't asking for them to change their mind, only to listen to some new facts that he had forgotten to include in his original presentation, facts that he thought might change the equation. Fred presented a great deal of information on his personal finances at the meeting . . . far more than anyone would normally reveal. The numbers showed that, despite being an executive in an Internet company, Fred wasn't the millionaire his fellow residents suspected. Fred also showed figures demonstrating the terrible impact on his personal finances of having to hold on to the apartment without renting. Fred then presented a note from the broker that not only reiterated the problems she had in trying to sell the unit but also estimated the price at which the unit would actually sell. The broker's note concluded by warning that a sale at that price would impact the value of all the building's units for years to come. In addition, the broker's note pointed out that forced transfers were becoming much more common and that, as a result, potential buyers might be scared off by the board's perceived inflexibility.

In conclusion, Fred made an impassioned plea. Instead of dwelling on his current situation, he focused on how much he hated to have to leave the area. He described his love for the building and the dreams he had of being part of the area's rebirth. By the end of his pitch the board's perception had changed. Fred was no longer a real estate speculator. He was someone just like them, facing a situation they might face if forced to move. Two days later he received permission to rent the apartment. Now, eighteen months later, he and the broker are about to put it back on the market.

ALEX LANDERS SAVED BY THE FEDS

If you looked at Alex Landers you'd never think she would be accused of insider trading. A forty-seven-year-old widowed mother of two teenagers, Alex is a biologist who has been doing medical research at the same major midwestern university for more than twenty-five years. A tall thin woman, with straight graying hair pulled back in a ponytail, Alex was clearly uncomfortable when she first came to my office. She apologized for her discomfort, admitting she felt more at home in jeans and a sweater than in the blue suit she was wearing. When she told me she had just been fired from the university for insider trading, my jaw must have dropped. Alex laughed out loud and started to explain.

Ever since she was an undergraduate, Alex had been working on biomedical research at the university. Her late husband had been a drama professor at the school. Both her children were undergraduates. She joked that she bled the school's colors. For more than fifteen years, Alex had been working on one particular research project. Early on, it had attracted little attention, but in the past five years, after she began publishing her preliminary results, it had become a hot topic. Eight months ago, after her third article appeared, a major pharmaceutical company had approached the university, offering to fully fund Alex's research, if they could have the rights to any medications that it generated. The university agreed.

Alex, grateful for the support from the corporation, thought it would be a nice gesture for her to support them too, and buy some shares in the company. She went to the broker that managed her retirement plan and had him purchase a block of stock. Six months after making the stock purchase, there was a breakthrough in Alex's lab. As always, she shared the news with her kids. Alex's oldest, Jeremy, who was a business major, suggested she buy more stock in the company since, after her article came out, it would probably go up in value. Proud of her son's ingenuity, Alex did just that, buying a second block of shares with more of her retirement funds. Jeremy's prediction was accurate. The day after Alex's report appeared in a scientific journal, the company's stock soared. The broker excitedly called Alex, explaining that her net worth had just jumped $25,000 overnight. Elated, a little mystified, and scared the windfall would vanish as quickly as it appeared, she told the broker to sell the stock.

Two days later she regaled her peers with the story at a staff meeting. The dean who managed the research program heard about it through the grapevine and called her into his office. He asked her if the basic facts he had heard were true. She said yes, asking what the problem was. He told her she was guilty of insider trading and was, as of that moment, terminated with no severance.

Alex was stunned. The university had been her whole life. She was able to afford to send her children to college thanks to the university providing subsidized tuition. Alex had never worked anywhere else. Now, not only didn't she have a job, but her entire support system had been severed. At the advice of a friend of hers in the business school, a professor I've interviewed for my writing in the past, she gave me a call.

Whatever the technicalities of the case, it seemed to me that the dean had overreacted. Alex's attempts to flesh out the story with the personal information that made her actions less nefarious had fallen on deaf ears. I knew she needed to ask for a reconsideration, and to do that, she needed more facts. After some thought we came up with an idea. I contacted a defense attorney I knew who had spent twenty years working for the Securities and Exchange Commission.

I told him the story and asked what he thought. He told me that though Alex seemed to be in technical violation of the statutes, it was also clear she simply had made a mistake. Considering the circumstances and the numbers involved, he said the SEC would have simply done some interviewing and then issued a warning.* He suggested that while Alex might be subject to termination, depending on the university's policies, her being fired for cause so promptly after twenty-five years on the job seemed an overreaction. He agreed to put his opinions in a letter.

Alex and I then sent that letter, along with a long memo from me outlining the situation, to the dean responsible for her firing, the uni-

---

*Please bear in mind that I've changed some of the facts of the case in order to protect my client's identity. The opinion the former SEC attorney offered was based on the facts in the real case, not those outlined here. In other words, don't use this case as an example of the SEC's opinions.

versity ombudsperson, ten other deans, the president, and the board of trustees. Three days after sending the package I received a call from the university's counsel. He offered Alex a settlement, giving her a year's paid leave of absence to find another position, and continued tuition subsidy for her children for the rest of their education. She accepted immediately. Four months later she was hired by the corporation that had been sponsoring her research.

Taking Charge of Your Life 9

Never underestimate a problem or your ability to cope with it. Realize that the problem you are facing has been faced by millions of human beings. You have untapped potential for dealing with a problem if you will take the problem and your own undeveloped unchanneled powers seriously. Your reaction to the problem, as much as the problem itself, will determine the outcome. I have seen people face the most catastrophic problems with a positive mental attitude, turning their problems into creative experience. They turned their scars into stars.

Robert H. Schuller

By learning and putting into practice my approach to business problem solving, you can achieve success. The obstacles you face in the course of your business or career that once seemed insurmountable barriers, can become little more than speed bumps. The nos that once seemed so powerful can now be shrugged off. Knowing how to turn no into yes gives you the ability to achieve goals that once seemed impossible. My approach won't make you an invincible negotiator or an infallible businessperson. No one is omniscient or omnipotent. But what it can do is almost as powerful.

Once you start following my approach and you begin to successfully turn no into yes you'll develop incredible self-confidence. When you know that you can overcome hurdles, you'll stop reining yourself in. Plans once deemed too risky or too fraught with peril will become viable. It's not that you'll become foolhardy; it's that you'll be more willing to take the measured risks that are required to achieve success. People "play it safe" in order to keep from facing obstacles, to keep from hearing no. But by never pushing their careers or businesses to the edge, they never fulfill their potential. Afraid of hearing a no, they never ask for as much as they could. Obstacles, problems, and nos are the wages of business and career progress.

When you stop being afraid of no, when you realize you can turn that no into a yes, you'll be free to ask for all you deserve. And only when you ask for it all can you get it. As Henry David Thoreau noted, "In the long run, men hit only what they aim at." If you're afraid of obstacles, if you're frightened by a no, you'll aim low, and as a result, you'll achieve little. If you're unafraid of obstacles, if you know you can turn no into yes, you'll aim high, and as a result, you'll achieve much. Confident in your ability to deal with the worst, you'll be free to press ahead and accomplish the best.

The ability to turn no into yes can make you fearless. Most if not all of our fears come from the unknown. We're frightened of what *might* happen, or what *could* happen. If we go into business for ourselves we *might* not be able to land clients. If we ask for a raise we *could* be turned down. We *might* not be able to get another job. We *could* end up in financial trouble. It's our fear of the unknown that turns mole-hills into mountains, and speed bumps into roadblocks.

But when you know how to turn no into yes the unknown stops being frightening. With the ability to turn around the worst thing that could happen—outright rejection—you gain the power to face anything. If a potential client says no, you can turn it into a yes. If your employer says no, you can turn it into a yes. You can cope with whatever comes your way. You can deal with any obstacles that appear. You can achieve all your business and career goals.

The ability to turn no into yes isn't just a business skill. While there are many personal nos that *should* be based on emotions, there are others that should not. If someone turns down your marriage proposal because he or she is not in love with you, it's wrong, even maybe dangerous, to try to turn that no around. Skills and abilities honed for the boardroom do not belong in the bedroom. However, they can work very well in the rest of the house. If you're facing obstacles in developing life or financial plans with your spouse, your children, or your parents, the ability to turn no into yes can help smooth relations and keep parties from polarizing. Divorce settlements and prenuptial agreements are, or at least should be, dealt with as financial issues, apart from their emotional overtones.

More importantly, the confidence and courage you develop from being able to overcome all your business obstacles will overflow into your personal life. When you lose your fear of the unknown in business, you'll also lose your fear of the unknown outside of business. Once you stop reining in your business life, you'll stop reining in your personal life. Personal plans once deemed too risky or too fraught with peril will become viable. You'll now be more willing to take the measured risks that are required to achieve personal as well as business success. People "play it safe" in their personal lives for the same reason they do in their business lives: to keep from facing obstacles; to keep from hearing no. By never pushing or daring to win in their personal lives, they never fulfill their potential. Once again, afraid of hearing a no, they never ask for as much as they could. Obstacles, problems, and nos are also the wages of personal progress.

Learn to turn no into yes and you can achieve not only all your business goals but all your personal goals as well. Confident in your ability to vault any hurdle, you'll lose the chains that have held you back from getting the most you can out of life. Freed of your fears, you can finally live the life of your dreams.

Reintroduction

I am, first and foremost, a personal advisor and counselor. I would never offer abstract advice on a client's approach to a problem without helping them apply it to their own business, career, financial, or personal situation. For the same reason, I would never offer a reader of mine advice without application.

The nine chapters you've just read are only part of what I do during my client consultations. In real life (as opposed to in books) I simultaneously explain my approach to problem solving and help a client work through his or her problem. That can't be done in the pages of a book, so I've been forced to split the process into distinct parts.

The rest of this book explains how to apply my problem-solving approach to the most common obstacles that face my clients. Each of the chapters replicates how, together, we would follow the checklist if you came into my office for help with a problem in a particular area of your money life. In each of the following chapters I've addressed the specific problems clients bring to me, in the language in which they're usually presented. My hope is that this will make it easier for you to find your own problems discussed. I have tried my best to make these chapters feel as much like a personal consultation as I could. They are forceful and succinct because that's the way I must be with clients who are paying by the hour. I hope they're also comprehensive and clear. However, if you find that anything I've written, no matter how trivial, is either confusing or incomplete, please don't hesitate to contact me.* Sometimes the best way to get a pertinent answer is to ask an impertinent question.†

---

*The best way to reach me is via E-mail at mark4smp@aol.com. If you're not online, you can write to me care of HarperBusiness.
†With apologies to Jacob Bronowski, who wrote, "That is the essence of science: ask an impertinent question, and you are on the way to a pertinent answer."

Part 2

Turning No into Yes When Facing Career Problems

Job Hunting   **10**

Come forth, Lazarus! And he came fifth and lost the job.

James Joyce, Ulysses

Job-hunting obstacles are often twin problems. In one incarnation they're expectant problems, representing fears of what could or might happen, such as, "they'll think I'm too old." Their other embodiment is as an extant problem, representing something that has already occurred, like, "they thought I was too old."

Interestingly enough, these twins aren't equivalents or even comparable; they're instead mirror images. In almost every case of twin job-hunting problems, the extant problem is the real issue and is entirely rational, while its expectant twin is a presenting problem that's completely emotional. If you're suffering from one of the expectant incarnations of the problems you'll need to go through most of the first five items on the checklist. On the other hand, if you're facing one of the extant twins you'll simply need to focus on an appeal.

Another common element to many job-hunting problems is that if you're forced to appeal a rejection, you'll have very little time to act. Today it's unlikely you'll hear you've been rejected, since usually only the successful candidate gets notified. If you think you did well, all you can do is sit and wait for a call. If you don't hear by the time indicated, call, ask what was behind the no, launch your appeal, and pray they haven't already given the job to someone else. If you sense during the interview that you're not coming across well, don't wait: decide yourself what is behind the soon to be coming no, and launch your appeal as soon as you get home. If you're unsure of how you did, try to find an inside source who can tip you off about your chances and let you know what was behind the no. Then jump back into the fray with your new facts and request for reconsideration.

I'm too old.

What's your problem?—Age is rarely ever the real problem in job hunting. If you're looking for work in a field in which physical strength and stamina are a factor—let's say roofing—age *can* be problematic. However, even in that case, your actual problem is you're looking for the wrong kind of job, not that you're too old. If physical strength and stamina aren't a factor in your work, then worries about age are indicative of a lack of confidence, enthusiasm, and/or motivation. You're blaming your age when it's your attitude that's the problem. Your real problem is you're bored, burned out, or unmotivated.

One problem at a time—Age fears may be disguising problem clusters or individual obstacles. If you're simply looking in the wrong business—you're looking for a roofing job when at this point you should really be selling roofing products—then it's a single problem. If, however, age fears are masking a poor attitude toward self or career, then it's likely you're facing a cluster.

In the latter case, the secret is to focus on the most pressing problem: that's eliminating outward signs of your being "burned out" so you can land a job that will then give you the time to work on the other elements in the cluster.

Focus on facts, not feelings—Unless you're a career sandhog or something similar, saying that your age will be a problem means you're focusing on feelings rather than on facts. To correct your focus ask yourself: what is making me feel old? and why have I lost my enthusiasm? Age should be an advantage, not a disadvantage. You have experience, wisdom, and sagacity. You're more responsible and less prone to mistakes. You may have slowed down physically, but thanks to your advanced knowledge and skill you can do in ten minutes what it would take someone without your experience ten days to do.

Become an expert—You can bolster your own confidence (and provide ammunition for a possible appeal) by finding out the ages of upper-level executives in the industry or company in which you're looking for a job. Is the president of the company older than you? Isn't he still competent? Is the most respected practitioner in your field the same age as you or older? Wouldn't she be a great candidate for this job?

In addition, become an expert on your own résumé. If you fear your age may keep you from landing an interview, consider pruning references that scream "veteran." You don't need to provide the year you graduated college, or include a comprehensive job history with dates. Your résumé can be a presentation of highlights. Stress your achievements, skills, and abilities rather than your career chronology. Prepare a separate job history and bring it with you to the interview.

Create an environment of trust—You don't need to pierce your eyebrow or dye your hair to convince someone else your age isn't an issue; you simply need to appear enthusiastic and energetic. Remember: your age isn't stamped on your forehead.

Use the full repertoire of trust-building techniques: smile, lean forward, be animated, ask questions, and actively listen. Don't act as if you've heard or done it all before, even if you have. Certainly don't treat an interviewer who's younger than you with any less respect. Use recent examples to illustrate your experience and abilities, not stories from before the information age. Take it from a seventy-year-old: enthusiasm takes at least ten years off your age and smiling takes off another ten. Come off as a dynamic, energetic candidate and no one will remember you voted for JFK.

Turn no into yes—If during an interview you suspect your age may be an issue, or just subsequent to the interview you learn from a source your age was a determining factor, you need to immediately telephone the interviewer. Apologize for your "less than stellar performance" and cite the personal problem or situation that caused your malaise and kept you from offering all your ideas. Ask for another meeting to present those new ideas. It's admittedly a long shot, since an age rejection is an emotional (and illegal) judgment rather than a rational decision. Still, it's worth a try. If they've already turned you down what more can they do?

What if I have to relocate?

What's your problem?—Fear about relocating is a presenting problem if you're single and without school-age children. That's because in that instance, relocation, while a chore, won't negatively impact your life. In fact, if you'll be getting a better job for more money it could positively impact your life. You're using relocation fears as a cover for your fear of change or some other worry about getting a new job.

If you're part of a couple and/or you have school-age children, relocation still isn't your real problem. Instead your obstacle is getting your employer to provide enough financial and other resources to make the transition less onerous for your family.

One problem at a time—Worries about the "costs" of relocation are almost always a cluster of related problems involving issues such as a spouse's career, a child's schooling, and extended family relations. The key is to isolate the individual problems and focus on solving each, realizing that financial compensation and employer counseling services can go a long way in solving all of them. Pick the most difficult problem first. For example, your spouse's hunt for a new job will be more difficult than your hunt for a new school for your daughter, or a new home. If you solve the most difficult problem, the others will subsequently be far more manageable.

Focus on facts, not feelings—If you're unmarried and/or don't have school-age children, fears of relocating are purely emotional. The fact is that you can fall in love with, or at least like, any location that offers you a chance to improve your career. If you do have spouse or child issues, relocating is a cluster of rational problems. However, they're probably not as difficult as you might at first perceive.

Become an expert—The more you and your family learn about your new location the less fearful you'll all be about the move. Carefully study the support and services your company offers for relocating employees. Look for any gaps or shortcomings in the package.

Create an environment of trust—Having obviously won the new job or promotion, you've already established a level of trust with your new employer. Maintain that trust by never showing hesitation about the move. Instead, simply ask for help in the parts of the package you've found lacking. Ironically, in this situation most employers will do more for an already committed employee than for one sitting on the fence. That's because they'll view further contributions as employee assistance rather than as job negotiation. Remember, by paying attention to the understandable concerns of your spouse and children you'll further secure your already trusting relationship with them.

Turn no into yes—You can try to appeal, or at least mitigate, decisions to relocate you by pushing for a possible flextime or telecommuting arrangement. However, I'd discourage the effort. Today, you really need to be willing to move where the work is.

I don't have enough education/experience.

What's your problem?—If it's a question of quantity—say the job calls for ten years' experience and you only have seven, or it calls for a master's degree and you only have a bachelor's—this is your actual problem. But, if it's a question of quality—perhaps you're worried your diploma isn't from Harvard or your experience is with a small firm—your real problem is a lack of confidence.

One problem at a time—Lack of sufficient education or experience is a single problem.

Focus on facts, not feelings—Don't focus on the quality of your education or experience; that's a subjective, emotional question. Instead, look at the objective nature of your education and experience as a total package. Experience can compensate for any lack of education, and education can compensate for a lack of experience. If you've already landed an interview, don't dwell on your insecurities; after all, your education and experience were good enough to get the interview. That means it's good enough to get you the job. If you're hesitating to apply for the job, don't presume to know more than the recruiter. Make your best objective case rather than giving in to your irrational fears.

Become an expert—Demonstrable expertise is the secret to overcoming this problem. Your education has made you an historian of the business. While you may not have personally lived through various events you know enough about them to have absorbed the same lessons as those who have experienced them. Similarly, your experience has offered the best possible education in the business. Your classroom has been the real world, and you've graduated from the school of hard knocks. These attitudes should come through on your résumé as well as in your conversation. Any third-party endorsements of your knowledge and professionalism, such as memberships in professional or trade associations, will help bolster your case.

Create an environment of trust—The more that you are able to generate trust during a job interview the easier you will be able to make the case that your education compensates for your lack of experience or vice versa.

Turn no into yes—If you've been turned down for lack of education or experience your only chance is to immediately ask for a reconsideration, based on your having forgotten to offer further examples of whatever was lacking. Maybe, because you were fighting off a cold, you forgot to mention that summer-long accounting program you took last year. Or perhaps, because you didn't realize its relevance, you failed to discuss the six months when you served as acting director of your department. The secret, as always, is to provide new facts, but to do it immediately, blaming yourself for the failure to include them earlier. This has worked on a number of occasions for clients of mine who acted promptly.

I don't have a network.

What's your problem?—Lack of a network is rarely a presenting problem. If you're really just afraid of looking for a new job you'd come up with a seemingly more difficult problem to overcome.

One problem at a time—This is a single problem.

Focus on facts, not feelings—This is a rational, rather than an emotional problem. Most jobs today are filled through personal contacts rather than ads.

Become an expert—The search for expertise is the perfect cover for developing a network of your own. Ask for informational interviews. Tap into your existing network, both personal and professional, to ask for the names of anyone, and I do mean anyone, who is connected to the industry or profession you're exploring. Your neighbor can give you the name and telephone number of his brother who's in the software business. Your accountant can introduce you to the name of the software consultant she used to set up her tax program. Never bring up jobs during these meetings. Instead, just ask for advice, information, and guidance about the business. You're on a quest for knowledge, not a job hunt. At the end of each meeting ask for the names of others who might be able to help you learn about the business. After a few months of these meetings you'll have the network you once lacked.

Create an environment of trust—This is one instance where it's what you don't say that matters most. If you indicate that you're really on a job hunt rather than a quest for knowledge you'll have lost any trust that your other efforts may have generated.

Turn no into yes—There's really no need to turn these nos into yeses. If someone refuses to meet with you to discuss their business, just thank them for their time and move on to the next name on your list.

What if they don't like me?

What's your problem?—Preinterview fear about the interviewer liking you is always a cover for a lack of confidence in your interpersonal skills. Your problem isn't "what if they don't like me," it's "my communication skills need work." On the other hand, if this is a postinterview fear, and you believe the other party didn't like you, it is your problem.

One problem at a time—Whether it's a presenting or actual problem, it's a single obstacle rather than a cluster or series.

Focus on facts, not feelings—If your fear of not being liked is expectant, you're being emotional. Focus on improving your interpersonal skills instead. If your fear of not being liked is extant, however, it's a rational problem you'll need to address directly.

Become an expert—Expertise, while always important, generally isn't a contributing factor in getting someone to like you.

Create an environment of trust—The shortcut to getting someone to like you is the same as the shortcut to getting someone to trust you: show them you care about them. If in garb, language, manner, and action you demonstrate your respect, concern, interest in, and appreciation of the other party, they should like you.

Turn no into yes—Notice I used the word *should* in the prior sentence. Unfortunately, there are instances when no matter what you do, you can't get someone to like you. There are people in the world who will dislike you for what you are, how you look, or where you came from, rather than who you are as an individual. It's disheartening, but even in business, a field in which judgments should be made based on the bottom line, there are people who will dislike you because of your religion, the color of your skin, or the place you were born. It's worthless to directly appeal to them for a reconsideration because their no is entirely irrational. No added facts can make a difference, since the no isn't based on facts.

Your only hope of turning such a no around is to appeal to a third party with a connection to the organization, asking them to intervene. Unfortunately, unless they're someone with influence over the person who rejected you, this effort is usually a forlorn hope. A discriminator will never admit his or her irrationality and can only be forced past their prejudice with internal pressures.

I've jumped from job to job.

What's your problem?—Job hopping is usually your actual problem. Your ability to repeatedly search for and land jobs demonstrates you're not afraid of job hunting and you're confident in your personal skills and abilities.

One problem at a time—If job hopping is uncommon in your business, then it's likely an umbrella for a cluster of problems dealing with your being in the wrong industry or profession. Rather than looking at your job hopping as the problem, try to determine the reasons for the job hopping. What are you looking for that you haven't found? Why do you leave your jobs? What is it about the new positions that entices you? If job hopping is common in your industry, then your excessive movement is a single problem . . . and not as much of one as you might fear.

Focus on facts, not feelings—Your job hopping is only an objective problem if it's uncommon in your industry or profession. If it's common practice, yet you're not happy about it, you're looking at it emotionally rather than rationally. If everyone else is job hopping too, then it won't be a problem for employers, and it shouldn't be a problem to you.

Become an expert—Obviously the key information to uncover is whether your job hopping is unusual in the context of your industry. If it isn't, then you've all the information you need to defend yourself against external or internal doubts. If it is, you need to research your own job history, demonstrating that each move has been a logical one, made to a position of greater responsibility. Analyze your own career to the degree that you can make a case for your movements being a logical progression.

Create an environment of trust—In a business in which people move around often, you'll never be able to generate sufficient trust for someone to believe you'll be there for the duration. All you can do is show your sincerity to stick around for as long as the job is rewarding and fulfilling. This isn't that big a deal, since in such a business no one expects any more from you. If you're in a business in which people don't shift jobs often, you'll need to pull out all the stops to demonstrate your belief that, after many years of searching, you've finally found a home.

Turn no into yes—If you're rejected because of excessive job hopping your best chance at turning the no around is to offer additional facts that demonstrate how this job fulfills your needs in ways previous jobs did not. However, as with all job-hunting problems, your time is short, since there are probably other qualified candidates.

I'm afraid I'll look stupid.

What's your problem?—This is never the real problem. In some cases it's just a cover for a poor self-image. In most instances, however, the real problem is the fear of making a mistake in the interview, fear of not having answers to every question.

One problem at a time—If it's a cover for a poor self-image then clearly it's a large personal cluster, not a single problem. But if it's just a mask for the fear of making a mistake, it's a single problem.

Focus on facts, not feelings—Framed as a personal failing, it's an emotional problem. Nothing you or anyone else can do will change feelings of stupidity. If you frame it instead as a quest to know all the answers to potential questions, then it's a rational problem. There's one caveat, however. You can go overboard and start worrying about absurd questions, like Richard Nelson Bolles's famous "What color is your parachute?" If that happens you've gone full circle and turned the problem back into an emotional rather than rational issue. Learn all you can, but don't feel like you're a failure if you haven't learned everything. That's an impossible mission.

Become an expert—Obviously, becoming an expert is the secret to solving this problem. The more you know about the person you're meeting with, the company you're approaching, and the industry it's in, the better you'll be able to field all questions.

Besides conducting the typical public and private research, I suggest you also carefully read a good newspaper for the week before the meeting. Make a note of any recent news events that could impact the business, for instance a change in interest rates. Not only will this insure you're on top of the latest concerns in your industry, but it will also give you something interesting to use as your own conversation starter.

Create an environment of trust—While it's essential to use all the trust-generating tools at your disposal, it's also important not to go too far in demonstrating your exhaustive research. You don't want to intimidate the other party with your knowledge, or come off as a know-it-all. Remember, just because you have the information doesn't mean you have to show it. Let it come out naturally. Even if you don't use it all, it will have helped you by boosting your confidence.

Turn no into yes—If, after an interview, you realize or learn you made a mistake, you need to correct it immediately. By fax or E-mail, send a note thanking the interviewer for his or her time, but also acknowledging your mistake or lack of knowledge, and demonstrating the new, correct information you've now acquired. Since you've already made a mistake you've nothing to lose by admitting it after the fact. By doing so you show humility and candor—two very valuable traits in employees—and by correcting yourself you show initiative—another excellent characteristic. It may not turn a job rejection into an offer, but it can't hurt.

Salary Issues

11

Money never cometh out of season.

Thomas Draxe

Most raise and salary problems, like job-hunting problems, are twins. First there's the expectant side to the problem: generally a fear that threatens to keep you from taking an action, such as "they're not going to give me any more money." And second there's the extant problem: an outright rejection, like "they said they won't give me any more money." However, unlike job-hunting problems, these twins are analogous. In fact, the secret to solving both sides of the dilemma is the same: expertise.

The key to being successful in initially asking for more money, or to appealing a negative decision about compensation, is to be an expert on the market value for what you do, and on how your personal value is perceived by the company. Even the most tightfisted organization in the world accepts that it must pay market value for good people. Therefore, the secret to getting more money is knowing you're valued and being able to demonstrate you're not receiving fair compensation for that value.

Though establishing trust between yourself and another party is vital in solving almost every problem, in raise and salary issues trust also takes on another role. You'll be presenting the expertise you've acquired on compensation. It's likely this will differ somewhat with the other party's notion of the market value. In order to solve your problem you'll need to generate trust *in your numbers*, as well as in yourself.

They're not going to give me any more money.

What's your problem?—If you're expecting a no because your employer's policy is to give only cost-of-living increases, this really is your problem. However, if you're trepidation is based on your own poor performance or the knowledge that you're already earning what you deserve, it's a presenting problem. In those cases your problems actually are "I don't merit a raise" and "they don't think I'm doing a good job."

One problem at a time—If this really is your problem then it's a single problem. But if you really have one of the other two problems I mentioned, you're facing clusters of career choice and job performance problems.

Focus on facts, not feelings—The fear of not getting a raise is quite rational today. Most companies now do everything they can to give no more than cost-of-living increases . . . and some are loath to do even that. Rightly or wrongly, staff is now seen by most companies as an expense rather than as an asset.

Become an expert—Expertise is the secret for getting a raise and appealing a raise rejection. I've found that the most effective argument for getting a salary increase in today's workplace is to say that you're not being paid market value for what you do. In effect, you're not being treated fairly, and if you were to leave, the company would have to pay any qualified replacement what you're asking for anyway. There are three important areas of expertise you need in order to make this argument successfully.

First, you need to analyze whether you're perceived positively or negatively by your superiors. Obviously, if you've had a recent review that will make the process simple. If you haven't been formally reviewed for a while, subtly check with your peers in the company. Review all your recent dealings with superiors and get a sense of how you were treated. You need to be honest with yourself. Don't sugarcoat or rationalize your feelings. Your gut instinct is probably right. If you determine you're not viewed as a top performer, asking for a raise isn't just foolish, it could be disastrous. In this case, your most pressing problem is really improving your superiors' opinions of you. If your analysis shows you are perceived to be an excellent employee you can continue on with your research.

Second, you need to accurately determine what the market value range is for your position. You can do this from both public and private research. Check with industry associations and trade magazines for salary surveys. Contact employment agencies and headhunters. Speak with your peers at other companies. Compile a written compensation survey, making notes of your sources. Once you learn what the salary range is for your position, compare it to your own compensation. Honestly ask yourself if you're currently being paid fairly. If you are about to start your second year as a marketing vice president and you are currently being paid at the lower end of the range, you actually don't have a complaint with your employer. Ask for a raise now and you'll mark yourself as presumptuous. If the market range isn't sufficient for your needs, your problem isn't getting a raise, it's that you're in the wrong industry or profession. However, if you're being paid below the range, or you've been in the job for five years and are still at the lower end, you deserve a raise.

Third, having determined that you're well thought of and are deserving of a raise, you need to investigate the company's finances and personnel policies. Does your employer seem to have the ability to pay market value for your job? Has your company in the past shown a willingness to pay people what they deserve, or have good employees moved on after reaching a certain pay level? If you discover your company isn't willing and able to pay market value for your services then your problem isn't getting a raise, it's finding a new job.

Create an environment of trust—If your superiors think well of you you've already created a good foundation of trust. In this situation, however, you need to create trust not only in yourself, but in your compensation survey. The more authoritative your survey, the more your superiors will trust your numbers. And if they trust your figures and want to be fair, they'll give you a raise. Make sure you cite reliable sources for all your estimates.

Turn no into yes—If all your expertise goes for naught and your raise request is turned down, there's still a way to turn that no into yes: get another job offer. It may sound drastic but it's entirely rational. Think about it: you've determined you're well thought of, aren't being paid market value, and your employer is able to pay you more, but your request has been turned down. That indicates you've nowhere else to go in that company . . . unless you can shake your company out of its complacency. An outside offer obviously gives you a chance for more money. It also throws two added facts into the equation that cry out for a reconsideration: some other company obviously disagrees with your employer and thinks you're being paid less than you deserve; and your value is even greater, now that you could be working for the competition. In such circumstances I've seen companies rebudget if necessary to keep valued employees. And if they don't, you can just accept the other offer.

If I ask for more they'll fire me.

What's your problem?—If you deserve a raise, this is a presenting problem masking your real obstacle: a lack of self-confidence. If you don't deserve a raise, this is your real problem.

One problem at a time—This is a cluster only if it's masking your poor self-image. Otherwise, it's a single problem.

Focus on facts, not feelings—Let's put the fears and emotions aside and look at the facts. If you're doing a good job, and aren't being paid what you deserve, how could anyone rationally take offense at your asking to be treated fairly and given more money? If your superior isn't rational, or your company doesn't believe in treating people fairly, what are you doing working there?

On the other hand, if you're already being paid market value, your superior is apt to get annoyed by your request for more money . . . I know I would. Still, that wouldn't lead to you being fired. You'd just be marked as someone with an inflated sense of their own value. Your current job is safe but you've probably blown any future you might have had.

Of course, if you're not doing a good job and you come and ask for a raise you could bring yourself real trouble. Asking for a raise based on poor performance indicates stupidity or a total lack of awareness or concern for the company's standards. While you might not get canned at that meeting you'll certainly rise to the top of the list.

Become an expert—Obviously, the key to solving or avoiding this problem is to determine whether or not you deserve a raise. If your performance is perceived as positive, if you're not being paid your market value, and if the company is able to pay a higher salary, then you will not get fired for asking for a raise. If your performance has been poor and/or you're already being paid what you're worth, asking for a raise could indeed bring you trouble.

Create an environment of trust—Not only do you need to have a level of trust already established with your superior, but you also need to back up your compensation survey with enough documentation so that your boss will trust your numbers.

Turn no into yes—If you somehow foul up, ask for a raise you don't deserve, and end up getting fired in the process, all hope isn't lost. However foolish your approach was, it didn't merit getting fired. That will be clear to any boss upon reflection. The secret to turning that no into a yes—at least until he comes up with another reason to fire you—is to give your boss some time. Don't launch into an immediate appeal. Leave his office and give him at least an hour to cool off. Then, return to his office. Don't accuse him of reacting irrationally, even though he did. Instead, apologize and ask him to reconsider. Say that you weren't aware of how bad your timing was, and that had you known you never would have asked. Humbly ask his forgiveness. Given a way to save face, odds are he'll take it. However, you'd be wise to start looking for another job immediately.

If I ask for more they'll take back their job offer.

What's your problem?—Generally this isn't a presenting problem. However, I have come across one or two people who have used this problem as a mask for their feeling that they don't deserve the job offer they've just received. For most people, however, this is their real obstacle.

One problem at a time—This is a single problem, not a cluster or series.

Focus on facts, not feelings—Phrased in this manner, the problem presents the other party as being more emotional than rational. A better way to look at this problem is to say, "If I ask for more, *and make my taking the job contingent on getting it,* they'll take back their job offer." In other words, it's only a rational problem if you push the other party into an either/or decision.

Become an expert—In order to solve this problem you need to know the market value range for the position. You can assume that since they're soliciting outside candidates for the job they're willing to pay market value. However, they may not know how much that is.

Create an environment of trust—As in most of the other raise/salary problem, you need to create trust in your numbers as well as in yourself, through citing reliable sources.

Turn no into yes—This whole problem is actually an appeal. You're asking the other party to reconsider their initial job offer. The first key to succeeding in your appeal is to make sure it's not framed in a confrontational manner. Say you're flattered by the offer, and are looking forward to the job. Rather than saying you need to resolve the money issue before accepting, act as if acceptance is already a given . . . even if it's not. Do that and you guarantee they won't take back their offer. Then, add that you do have a problem with the initial salary offer and need their help in solving it. Explain that you know they want to be fair and that you're sure they weren't intending to offer less than the market value to you, but according to your own research, they'd done just that. Then offer up your compensation survey and ask them to reconsider their offer based on the new information you're presenting. Don't be surprised if their response is to settle midway between your figures and their initial offer.

They gave me a raise . . . but it wasn't enough.

What's your problem?—This is a real problem. Many employers know that by giving modest unsolicited raises they can preempt raise requests, which might result in their having to pay more. Most employees, having been given a raise, feel guilty going back and asking for more. You shouldn't be. If the impromptu raise doesn't bring you up to the market value for your position, experience, and skills, then you're still not being paid fairly.

One problem at a time—This is a single problem, not a cluster or series.

Focus on facts, not feelings—Don't focus on your feelings of gratitude for the raise. Instead, concentrate on the fact that you're still not being paid what you're worth.

Become an expert—As always in raise and salary situations, you need to become an expert in the market range for your position and your company's ability to pay fair wages.

Create an environment of trust—And again, you need to generate trust not only between you and your employer, but also trust in your numbers.

Turn no into yes—This situation is similar to asking for a larger initial salary. The entire process is an appeal. Stress your gratitude for the raise. Explain that you're flattered and are enthusiastic about your future with the company. But note that you have a problem you need help in resolving.

Say that while you know it wasn't intentional (even though it probably was), the salary offered amounted to little more than a cost-of-living increase, and didn't bring you up to the market level for what you do. Ask for a reconsideration based on the new facts you're presenting about the standard compensation for someone like you. As in the initial salary discussion, be prepared for a compromise settlement.

Employment Contracts

12

A verbal contract isn't worth the paper it is written on.

Sam Goldwyn

You'd think problems about contracts would, by and large, be very clear and rational. Actually, after spending a great deal of time in the past four or five years working on employment contract problems, I've discovered that most of the situations brought to me are presenting problems, and quite a few of them are framed in emotional, rather than rational, terms. I think that's because rather than being primarily contract problems, they're actually employment problems. Since so much of our self-image today is tied up in our career, when an effort is made to codify our work world, we take it very personally. In defining the terms of our employment we think we are, in some way, defining ourselves. But we're not.

The key to overcoming most of the obstacles related to employment contracts is to look at them dispassionately. Formal written contracts have become commonplace as a result of the tearing up of the informal unwritten contract of the past. Since doing your job no longer guarantees you'll keep your job, and doing your job well no longer insures you'll get a raise or be promoted, employees have had to become more flexible. This willingness to jump ship has led employers to push valued staff to sign contracts in order to keep them from working for the competition—now and in the future—and to get a handle on their current and future payroll. Shifting jobs in midcareer has led employees to ask for contracts in order to formally obtain the security they once had by virtue of their long tenure at a company. In order to solve employment contract problems it's essential to focus on these rational needs of both parties, rather than the attached emotional and psychological issues.*

You'd also think that expertise would be very important to solving these problems. Yet actually, it's not your expertise that counts. Sure, you need to know your value on the open market. But beyond that, most of the expertise, for both sides, will be provided by hired guns: the lawyers.

If I ask for a contract they'll take back their job offer.

What's your problem?—This is never the real problem facing one of my clients. Sometimes, having an employment contract *should* be a quid pro quo for taking a job. For instance, if you're in midcareer and you're relocating to take a new position you should receive some contractual security in exchange for uprooting yourself and your family. Or, if you're being recruited to leave a wonderful job that you love, you should receive some recompense for the tenure you're losing. In either of those situations you shouldn't even worry about their taking back an offer in response to a contract request. Instead, you should be grateful if they make your decision so easy. In effect, your problem really is that you're jumping too quickly at a job offer that might not be right for you.

If you're not relocating, or you're potentially leaving a less than desirable job or one you're unhappy with, this still isn't you actual problem. Rationally you should know that, at your level, asking for a contract is quite common nowadays. It will simply be seen as part of the standard compensation negotiation. This isn't a line in the sand unless you draw it yourself. Your real problem is you're afraid that, by asking for a contract, you'll lose the trust you generated in the interview process. You're worried they'll think you're potentially disloyal or not a team player.

---

*In this chapter, I'll be looking at contracts from the employee's side of the table. In a subsequent chapter, I'll be looking at them from the employer's side.

One problem at a time—This is a single problem rather than a cluster or series.

Focus on facts, not feelings—Rather than seeing the employment contract as somehow defining you as a human being, focus on it as being the only way today for employers and employees to achieve the kind of mutual security they need to prosper.

Become an expert—Other than your market value, the only real expertise you need to obtain is that you're not the only person in your profession or industry who has ever asked for a contract.

Create an environment of trust—Here's the secret to success. Rather than framing your request as a sine qua non for taking the job, treat it as part of the compensation negotiation. Begin by reiterating your excitement at starting work, and once again express your thanks. Then, explain that, since you have a family and you're leaving a job where you had tenure, you'd like some security. Ask for a contract that guarantees you a certain term of employment and a defined compensation package, an agreed-to salary protection in case you're terminated without cause. Framing the contract as protection for your family, not as a requirement for taking the job, lets you maintain the trust you've built up with your new superior.

Turn no into yes—If framing the request in this manner isn't sufficient to get approval, you can still appeal. Ask for a reconsideration, based on a new request, this time, for a termination agreement rather than an employment contract. This is more than just a language difference. A termination agreement deals specifically with what compensation you'd receive if you were fired without cause. It doesn't address the terms of your employment, your job description, or your current and future compensation. All it covers is what kind of severance package you'll receive if you're let go.

The other party will probably say that he would never fire you without cause. Agree immediately, but note that you can't rely on his successor being as trustworthy.

I've had a great deal of success in getting otherwise recalcitrant employers to sign termination agreements. For my clients, and for most employees, they achieve the most important goal: security. Being assured of two years' severance upon termination is just as good as having a contract for two years' employment.

If I try to negotiate the contract they're suggesting, they'll think I'm disloyal.

What's your problem?—This is also always a presenting problem. Your real problem is that you're afraid they'll blame you in case negotiations become thorny or protracted.

One problem at a time—This is a single problem, not a cluster or series.

Focus on facts, not feelings—Don't focus on the contract negotiation as being a confrontation between you and your superior; it's not. In offering a legal document for you to sign, your superior and her company have to assume that you will be showing that agreement to an attorney and getting some advice. They also assume that, once a lawyer looks at a document, there will be a negotiation over its terms and language. That's why they have their own lawyer standing by to negotiate. Rather than a surprising and potentially disruptive and disconcerting negotiation between you and your superior, the negotiation over the terms of an offered employment contract is anticipated and expected to fall into the hands of the lawyers. Your employer won't think you're disloyal. At worst, they'll think you have a fool for a lawyer.

Become an expert—There's no need for you to be an expert on employment contracts; that's why you hire a lawyer. In fact, not being an expert allows you to distance yourself from the negotiation. In the event of a stalemate you can always come in yourself to clean things up.

Create an environment of trust—By letting the lawyers on both sides handle the terms of the contract, you and your employer can both maintain the mutual trust that has developed during the interview process.

Turn no into yes—This entire problem is actually an appeal, since the first draft of a contract is really an initial offer. It's also an appeal you can leave in the hands of your lawyer.

If I sign a contract, I'll be stuck in this job and this salary.

What's your problem?—Of all the usual employment contract problems brought to me by clients this is the one that *isn't* a presenting problem.

One problem at a time—This is a single problem, not a cluster or series.

Focus on facts, not feelings—You're being entirely rational in seeing a contract offer in this way. It is an effort to do exactly what you see as the problem. Your employer wants to lock you into this job and at this pay . . . that's why he's asking you to sign the contract.

Become an expert—Here's the one contract problem where you need to develop some expertise . . . but about compensation, not contracts. The legal issues can be left to the lawyers. You need to determine what the market value range is for your job, where you stand today in relation to that range, and where you should be in that range during the term of the contract.

Let's say you learn that an account executive in your industry earns anywhere from $75,000 to $100,000. If you just became an accountant executive last year, and the offered contract provides you with a salary of $77,000, that is fair . . . initially. However, if it's a five-year contract offering you nothing more than annual cost-of-living increases during those five years, it isn't fair. Arguably, in those five years your market value would be increasing. In your third year, for instance, you might be worth $87,500. And in your fifth year you could be worth the full $100,000.

Create an environment of trust—Having determined how this contract would affect your being paid market value for what you do, you next need to get your employer to trust your numbers. That means citing reliable sources for your numbers, just as if you were asking for a raise or a higher initial salary. Don't worry about the level of trust that exists between you and your employer. If she didn't trust you she wouldn't want to bind you to her legally.

Explain to your superior that you have no problem "marrying" the company. In fact, you're excited by the possibility of having a long-term future with the firm. However, you have a problem. You're sure the company has mistakenly failed to provide compensation that would keep you within the market value range for your position. All you're asking for is fairness.

Turn no into yes—If your petition for fairness earns a rejection, you can still appeal. In this case, your request for a reconsideration should be based on a change in the term of the contract. For instance, the new fact you're injecting into the discussion is that you'd be prepared to sign a three-year deal that brought you up to $87,500, rather than a five-year deal that brings you up to $100,000.

Promotions

13

Advancement often depends not on rightness of action, but on acceptable behavior and image, e.g., self-control, appearance and dress, perception as a team player, style and patron of power.

Robert W. Goddard

Obstacles to getting a job promotion are probably the most straightforward career problems. There are two basic problems: one expectant and one extant. Rarely is either ever used as a mask for another problem. They are completely rational. And thankfully, both have equally straightforward solutions.

My current boss will think I'm disloyal.

What's your problem?—If you're looking to move to a position in which you report to a different superior, this is almost always a real problem. In my experience, if you were masking an ego problem you'd in all likelihood use yourself as an excuse rather than your boss.

One problem at a time—This is a single problem, not a cluster or series.

Focus on facts, not feelings—Rather than your boss's feelings, what's actually at issue here is his willingness to support your request, or at least not stand in your way.

Become an expert—Do some research and thinking and develop a plan that will let you take the new position without it hurting your current boss or his department. This could involve offering suggestions for temporary or permanent replacements, or even offering to do double duty until your replacement is up to speed. The key is to be able to placate any and all of your current superior's legitimate concerns.

Create an environment of trust—The secret to overcoming potential objections from your current boss is to focus on the personal, rather than business, trust that has developed between the two of you. Make it clear that you're coming to him as a friend, asking for help, not as a subordinate, asking for consent. Thank him for all that he has done for you as a person, not just as an employee. The idea is to make it difficult for him, as a friend, to stand in the way of your bettering your career. Few superiors, when faced with such a personal appeal, will feel they can be openly selfish enough to stand in your way.

Turn no into yes—That doesn't mean your superior won't try to keep you from jumping to another job. All it means is that he'll look for some practical reason for keeping you. Since you'll have developed the expertise to eliminate all the roadblocks to your current job's continued smooth operation, a recalcitrant boss will instead turn to your qualifications. Despite years of encouragement and positive reviews, you're apt to now hear criticism of your skills and abilities. You could be told you're not ready, or you're not up to the new challenge. The secret to this appeal is that it's really a nonappeal. Say that you're surprised to hear such criticism, but that you have to respectfully disagree. Explain that you'll be leaving that judgment up to your boss's boss. Remember: you didn't come to him for his permission, just his support. If he won't support your promotion campaign simply let his boss know that he's loath to lose you. That way, your current boss's intransigence could do more for your image than even his support.

They turned down my request.
What's your problem?—Obviously, this isn't a presenting problem.
One problem at a time—It's also a single problem, rather than a cluster or series.
Focus on facts, not feelings—And it's also entirely rational.
Become an expert—Assuming you've already gained sufficient knowledge to campaign for the position, the only further expertise you'll need comes from your appeal.

Create an environment of trust—Again, since you'll have already established trust during your past job history, and in the interview process, all you'll need to do is continue showing the utmost respect for the process and the people involved.

Turn no into yes—The entire solution to this problem is an appeal. First, look behind the no to find out why you were turned down. Don't ask for the reason in a confrontational manner. Instead, present it as part of your ongoing program of self-improvement. Ask what your deficiencies were so you can work on them in the future.

Once you're given a reason for the rejection you can ask for a reconsideration based on new facts that you're providing which directly bear on that reason. For example, if you're told you don't have sufficient computer expertise, you can explain that you'd forgotten to make it known you'd taken two summer courses in just the kind of technical problems you would be facing.

One note of warning: if you're told the reason for your not getting the position is that another candidate was more qualified, do not criticize the winner. Instead, ask what there is about the winner that set her apart from you. Explain that you'd like to know, so in the future you can be as good a candidate as she was. Make note of the information for future use, but don't launch into an immediate rebuttal or try to show how you are equally qualified. Any further efforts you make at promoting your own candidacy, no matter how honest or evenhanded, will be seen as sour grapes and an attack on the successful candidate. This is one instance when an appeal would clearly backfire.

Terminations 14

"You're fired!" No other words can so easily and succinctly reduce a confident, self-assured executive to an insecure, groveling shred of his former self.

Frank P. Louchheim

It's not surprising that termination problems are among the most disturbing hurdles my clients face. I know it's of no consolation at first, but it's important to understand that termination fears, while understandable, are really irrational. They are almost all expectant fears—after all, you've already been fired—and are actually fairly simple to overcome.

In the more than two decades that I've been a personal consultant I've been involved in hundreds of termination negotiations, some quite acrimonious and a few of which ended up in litigation. Yet, in all that time I have never seen a legitimate initial severance offer taken off the table after an effort was made to negotiate it upward. And I have never heard of a company giving a negative reference to someone who was fired without cause. In fact, I've never even heard of someone who was fired *for* cause actually being given a "bad" reference.

Having had the ground cut out from under them, few people realize just how powerful they are in a termination scenario. Think about it for a minute. What is an employer's leverage over an employee? His job. Once an employer fires you, there's literally nothing more he can do to you. He is now powerless over you. It's you who now has all the leverage. It is in your power, not the employer's, to make the process quick and clean, or long and dirty. You hold all the best cards, albeit in a losing game. Recognize that, and you'll be able to play your hand for all it's worth.

They'll take back their first offer if I try to negotiate severance.

What's your problem?—This is clearly your real problem. Fear of rejection usually doesn't matter anymore, since you've already received the ultimate workplace rejection.

One problem at a time—This is a single problem, unless you choose to bring in elements other than money—like outplacement assistance, COBRA, or continued use of office facilities—and turn it into a cluster.

Focus on facts, not feelings—Try as best you can to set aside your anger and fear over having been terminated. Focus instead on the facts of your situation. You have all the power now, since they have wielded their ultimate weapon and you are still alive. There is nothing more they can do to you. Yet, there's a lot more you can do to them.

The company wants you to leave as quietly and quickly as possible. Everything they are and will be doing is designed to speed you out the door. Do not read this pressure as being a threat to give you no severance, unless they specifically say it is a take-it-or-leave-it offer. And even if they do that, don't let it lead you to surrender. Instead, bypass the rest of the problem-solving checklist and move immediately to the appeal process.

Having been told that you're terminated, you'll be pushed to immediately agree to a package that's offered and pack up your office and leave. Refuse to sign anything, saying that you're in no mental or emotional state to rationally go over the papers being shoved in front of you. Agree to leave only after you have an appointment to speak about the severance package two or three days later.

Become an expert—In the two or three days available to you prior to the next meeting you need to become an expert on the job market. Contact headhunters, peers, employment agencies, industry journalists, and your professional association. Ascertain how long it takes, on average, for someone of your age, experience, and salary to find a new position *comparable* to the one you've left.

Employers will always cite the booming economy as a reason to offer little severance. However, you're not going to be looking for a job stuffing tacos at Taco Bell; you want an upper-level executive job at Pepsico's corporate headquarters. Fairness requires you to get enough severance to keep you afloat long enough to find a comparable job, not just any job.

In addition, if there is any possibility that your termination is tainted by discrimination based on gender, age, disability, sexual orientation, race, religion, marital status, or national origin, add a professional's expertise to your arsenal. For better or worse, the knowledge that you, as a protected minority, have hired legal counsel to examine the circumstances of your termination will set off alarm bells all over your company's offices. Your severance package, never etched in stone to begin with, has just become as malleable as water.

Create an environment of trust—If you're not a member of a protected minority you'll have to rely on the issue of fairness. Rather than letting your quick job market survey stand on its own, look to create an advocate.

Turn to the person who was your mentor in the company . . . even if she was the one who wielded the ax. Contact her at home, if possible. Explain how you've always looked to her as more than just a business mentor. Solidify the bond of personal trust that has developed between you over your tenure at the company. If she was the one who fired you, say that you know that was strictly business. This conversation, on the other hand, is personal. Then, tell her the results of your research, explain that you'll need more severance to bridge the gap in your employment, and ask her, as a friend, to put in a good word for you.

Personnel offices will do all they can to stick to company policy . . . unless some other executive gives them a reason to make a break with policy. Basically, they need to have someone else to blame for the exception they'll be making. The expertise you've acquired, and the prodding from an advocate, should be enough to boost your severance package.

Turn no into yes—But if you're still faced with a no, or if you're originally confronted by a take-it-or-leave-it offer, you'll need to move up the ladder. Your appeal needs to be in writing, either by letter, fax, or even E-mail, sent to the highest executive in the company you can approach. Don't feel uncomfortable going over others' heads . . . what can they do to you? Describe the situation as clearly and concisely as possible, and ask for a reconsideration based on the facts that you've uncovered about the job market. State that you know the company would never knowingly act unfairly, and that you hope these new facts will shed light on the matter.

What if they give me a bad reference?

What's your problem?—This is only a presenting problem if you're feeling guilt over having done such a bad job that you deserved to be fired, or if you really are in an industry—such as day care—in which positive references are essential. In the latter case your problem really is "what if they don't give me positive reference." In every other situation this is an actual, if irrational, problem.

One problem at a time—This is a single problem, not a cluster or series.

Focus on facts, not feelings—Companies today are so worried about possible litigation that they generally refuse to give any reference, other than stating that someone indeed worked for the company for a stated period of time. That goes even for people who were fired for cause. Some organizations may provide additional details, such as job titles, but few, if any, will offer any subjective comments.

Become an expert—The only real expertise you need in this case is the knowledge that a negative reference is very unlikely, and that severance packages are negotiable, giving you an opportunity to ask for a positive reference as part of your package.

Create an environment of trust—While the trust you generated on the job wasn't sufficient to keep you from being terminated, reinforcing it with a personal meeting and conversation might be enough to insure that your superior will be willing to write and sign a positive reference letter.

Turn no into yes—Generally, requests for a positive reference are turned down for reasons of company policy. The best way to turn that no around is to ask your superior to instead write a personal letter of reference, as a favor from one friend to another.

Part 3

Turning No into Yes When Facing Small-Business Problems

Seed Money   **15**

"My boy," he says, "always try to rub up against money, for if you rub up against money long enough, some of it may rub off on you."

Damon Runyon

Providing seed money to a business is the riskiest investment around. That's why no institution will ever make such an investment. Instead, entrepreneurs must turn to family, friends, and their own resources to come up with the initial funds for a business start-up. Only people who know you very well are going to take this kind of a risk and help fund your new business.

In some ways, asking friends and relatives for money is even more demanding than approaching institutional lenders. Banks and venture capitalists have clear-cut lending and investing formulas, which they'll make available to anyone who's interested. Your proposal will either fit the institution's criteria or not. Private investors and lenders, on the other hand, have far more complex and varied individual guidelines for investing. As a result, your proposal and pitch will need to be customized for each and every potential private investor.

Reducing risk is extremely difficult, if not impossible. In order for you to mitigate your friends' and family's fears you'll need to become an expert, not only on your own business, but on their needs and wants too. You must be as heavily invested personally in the business as possible. In other words, you've got to put your own money, or house, where your mouth is. Your business plan and loan proposal must both be able to withstand rigorous analysis and fit the unique needs of the potential investor as well. And even with all the expertise in the world you'll still need to develop an incredible level of trust. Having a personal relationship with the other party will have given you a head start, but you'll need to translate the trust they may have in you as a friend, or nephew, into trust in you as a businessperson.

In my years of consulting with entrepreneurs I've found that every expectant fear about raising seed money is actually a presenting problem. The only actual obstacle facing a person in search of seed money is the obvious extant problem: you've been turned down.

They won't give me the loan.

What's your problem?—This is the one actual problem in raising seed money for a small business.

One problem at a time—While more than one reason for the rejection may be cited initially, that's almost never, in fact, the truth. For every potential lender or investor there's a single deciding factor. That makes this, despite initial appearances, always a single problem.

Focus on facts, not feelings—Clearly, if you need the money, this is a rational problem. What's important is that, despite the personal relationship you share with the other party, you don't let emotional issues come into play. For the investment or loan to work for both of you, it must be sought and given on purely impersonal terms. The bond between the two of you must remain an unspoken subtext and never become the subject of discussion. Treat their rejection as entirely rational, even if you suspect it may have emotional underpinnings, and you'll be able to turn it around.

Become an expert—Before even asking for the loan or investment you should have made sure you were an expert in the industry you were entering, and in the specific business you were planning to launch. You also need to know your business plan and loan proposal like the back of your hand. If you have to check the text for the numbers to answer basic questions you're not expert enough. All of this information must be openly demonstrated for the other party to have confidence in you.

Expertise on the other party's wants and needs, however, shouldn't be flaunted. Instead, it should be used as the basis for your proposal. Your pitch should appear to be tailor-made for them . . . because it is. Remember the example I gave earlier in the book where a relative would not loan money because of a bad experience he had with another relative who never paid him back? Becoming an expert means becoming an expert, not only on your business plan, but also on the motivations/feelings of those you are asking for the loan. The amount you ask for, and their planned exit, should perfectly fit their current financial plan.

Create an environment of trust—Let the trust you have built up in your personal relationship remain in the background. It should serve as an invisible foundation for all the traditional business techniques you would use to create trust in someone you had never met before. You should dress and act the same in pitching Aunt Daisy as you would Citibank. Do any less and you'll appear to be a less than serious businessperson who is taking the other party for granted. That's not someone to trust with your money.

Turn no into yes—The secret to reversing a no from a friend or family member is the same as if it came from a banker or venture capitalist. You must first look behind the no and learn the reason for it, and then you need to ask for a reconsideration based on new facts that directly rebut the given reason.

One advantage of asking friends and family for seed money is that it's easy to subsequently ask them for the reason for their rejection. The problem is they may not feel comfortable telling the truth. You'll need to stress the importance "for your future efforts" of your getting the truth, and you'll also need to be able to read between the lines. Remove all the euphemisms and camouflage and you'll find that there are really only three reasons why a friend or family member wouldn't give you seed money: they don't think your business will succeed, they don't trust your ability or character, or they don't have the money.

If anyone says the reason they rejected your proposal is they didn't like your business plan, then they should be asked for specifics. Say that you respect their opinion and want to see if you can overcome their problem. If they can't offer any specifics, their real reason is something else. However, if they cite a particular element of the plan, offer additional facts that either dispel their fear or clear up their misconceptions.

If you're told the reason for a rejection is lack of funds, you've either made a mistake in your earlier research into their finances, or they're covering up another reason. You can find out which is the case by asking them to become a loan guarantor rather than an investor or lender. If the only reason for their rejection was that they didn't have money available, they'll likely agree. If they continue to balk, then their real reason is something else, probably a lack of trust.

A friend or family member is unlikely to come right out and say that they don't trust your skills or abilities. Instead, they'll initially offer other reasons, and then when pressed, raise vague questions. "Are you sure you know what you're doing?" they'll ask. "Do you really think that's the business for you?" they'll wonder. Alternatively, if they're concerned with your character they're apt to cite some irrefutable rules like "I never lend money to relatives," or "I never invest in retail businesses."

Since your recent efforts at establishing trust in yourself as an entrepreneur, coupled with the personal trust you had built up during your prior relationship, weren't enough to overcome their worries about you, it's unlikely you'll be able to turn them around yourself. Instead, ask if you can come back to them later, after you've lined up other investors or lenders. Then, your request for a reconsideration can be based on the demonstrable new facts of there being others who trust you enough to invest in your future.

I'm worried they won't like my idea (or) **I'm afraid they won't think I can do it.**

What's your problem?—These, like all other expectant obstacles about raising seed money, are presenting problem. Your real problem is that you don't sufficiently like your idea or that you don't think you can do it.

One problem at a time—This is a single problem.

Focus on facts, not feelings—What is it that you don't think they'll like about your idea? Odds are that's what you're not sure of yourself. What is it that they'll think you can't do? Turn the problem into a specific complaint or fear rather than a general worry. For example, "I'm worried they won't like my idea of relying entirely on Internet sales rather than a storefront," or "I'm worried they won't have confidence in my ability to manage money."

Become an expert—You need to start over, from scratch, and reeducate yourself about your business plan, beginning with the specific example you came up with earlier. But don't stop with just that one item or concept. Validate every assumption. Run all your cash flows again. Check your revenue and expense projections. Do another round of market research. Unless you have total confidence in your plan, no one else will.

Create an environment of trust—Since this problem is inside your head, the trust you need to create is internal as well. Hopefully, developing more expertise will lead to greater self-confidence.

Turn no into yes—If after reeducating yourself you're still unconvinced of your idea or your ability to carry it out, don't bother conducting an internal appeal. Either you're looking at the wrong business or you just don't have the personality to be an entrepreneur.

I'm afraid they'll steal my idea.

What's your problem?—This is a presenting problem. Your real problem is that you're afraid of rejection.

One problem at a time—This is a single, albeit irrational, problem.

Focus on facts, not feelings—Let's look at this realistically for a moment. In order to get someone to lend you start-up money you're going to have to develop incredible expertise, create professional as well as personal trust, and in the process jump through hoops, stand on your head, and juggle three balls. All this to get them to invest just a portion of the money needed to start the business. Yet you're afraid that just by hearing your idea all those barriers to investing or lending that they have will immediately crumble and they will want to invest all the time and money involved in starting the business. You're worried your Aunt Sadie will become not just an entrepreneur but an unethical one at that.

Become an expert—If through your research you've learned that your Aunt Sadie is actually a combination corporate raider/predatory entrepreneur then you have a right to be afraid.

Create an environment of trust—If you feel that you can't trust your friends and family, then perhaps you should jump ahead to part 5 of this book, which deals with overcoming personal problems.

Turn no into yes—There's no need to appeal a nonexistent problem.

Buying a Business 16

The buyer needs a hundred eyes, the seller not one.
George Herbert, Jacula Prudentum

Problems in buying an existing business are never really what they first seem. Worries about trusting the seller's numbers are actually concerns over your own accountant's competence. A seller's demand for an all-cash deal is really a smoke screen for her lack of trust in you or your expertise. And your fears about not having sufficient information to make a sound decision are masks for your own lack of confidence.

I don't trust her numbers.

What's your problem?—Since all you have to go on in making an analysis of a business are the numbers provided by the seller, not being confident in them is a definite problem. However, a competent accountant, with experience in analyzing small businesses similar to the one you're investigating, should be able to provide you with all the insight you need. That's why I've found that when a buyer expresses a lack of trust in the seller's numbers, what he's actually worried about is his own accountant's ability to validate those numbers.

One problem at a time—This is a single problem.

Focus on facts, not feelings—If you've hired a skilled, experienced accountant who was recommended by individuals you trusted, then you're being irrational in worrying about the seller's numbers. The facts you should focus on are your accountant's credentials.

Become an expert—Sure, you should be an expert in the business you're looking to purchase. And it's important to be an expert in the financial end of the industry you're entering. However, that doesn't mean you also need to be an expert in auditing and placing a value on businesses. Become an expert in the areas important to you and your future success. And hire an accountant who is an expert in the areas that pertain only to this transaction.

Create an environment of trust—There are many creative ways to mitigate your lack of trust in a seller. For instance, the seller could take back paper equal to any amounts in question, or could serve as a consultant long enough for the buyer to learn the minute details of the business and to make sufficient money to pay off the full purchase price. With all these techniques available, you should instead focus on developing trust in your accountant, and getting the seller to trust in your ability to run the business. The former will insure you're making a sound purchase, and the latter will insure you'll get the best terms.

Turn no into yes—Appeals don't really apply to the purchase of an existing business. If your accountant cannot validate the numbers offered as grounds for the selling price there's no reason to appeal. Offer the amount the numbers show the business to be worth and no more.* If the seller refuses, and cannot either certify or explain the questionable numbers, walk away from the deal.

The seller won't take back paper.

What's your problem?—While this is an actual problem for you, it is a presenting problem for the seller. It is almost always to a seller's advantage to not be paid all in cash, since that would result in a large tax bill. In addition, a seller can generally get a higher price if she is willing to take back paper. A demand for all cash is really a cover for

---

*The business's tax returns and the expression of its value are very often different. Sellers will be the first to try to reconcile the two different sets of numbers. A good accountant will make them prove their assertion of value and will know how to examine the seller's business and personal records to determine exactly what really is the value of the business.

the seller's lack of trust in your ability to run the business. She wants to get all her money now, because she thinks you'll run it into the ground.

One problem at a time—This is a single problem.

Focus on facts, not feelings—This is an entirely rational problem. You need to muster all the facts you can about your expertise and skills and use those to change the seller's feelings.

Become an expert—Clearly, you either haven't become sufficiently expert enough in the business, or you haven't successfully demonstrated your expertise.

Create an environment of trust—If your own efforts at creating trust haven't worked, try to enlist the aid of third parties. Speak with your contacts at major suppliers, local banks, the chamber of commerce, or trade associations and ask them to share their confidence in you with the seller. Try directly asking the seller what you could do to make her feel better about the deal.

Turn no into yes—Rather than launching a direct appeal of this problem, treat it as another negotiating ploy. Respond with a different offer while further demonstrating your expertise and having third parties endorse your skills and character. If this three-pronged approach can't move the seller off her demand for all cash she really doesn't want to sell.

Do I really have what it takes to run the business?

What's your problem?—This isn't just an actual problem, it's a self-fulfilling prophecy. If you don't feel that you know enough to manage the business then you don't.

One problem at a time—This is a single, albeit significant, problem.

Focus on facts, not feelings—This is a rational problem if you don't feel you have sufficient experience and expertise. If, on the other hand, you've already managed a similar business for ten years and arguably you have all the knowledge you need, you're being irrational. You're just afraid of taking the risk.

Become an expert—Whether this is a rational or emotional problem, the key is to go back and redouble your efforts at becoming an expert. Leave no stone unturned. Read everything you can. Talk to everyone you can think of. Run your numbers again. Reanalyze your market studies. If you still don't feel confident after all that, the problem is within you: you're simply not an entrepreneur.

Create an environment of trust—The trust you need to generate here is within yourself. If you're not satisfied with your own efforts, ask other unbiased parties for their advice. Speak with your attorney, accountant, and banker. Ask them if they think you have what it takes to run this business. Perhaps you'll trust their judgment more than your own.

Turn no into yes—Actually, this entire process is an internal appeal of a self-rejection. The new facts you're adding are more expertise and outside opinions. If they're not enough to change your own mind, let the matter drop.

Buying a Franchise

17

If you're going to sin, sin against God, not the bureaucracy. God will forgive you but the bureaucracy won't.

Admiral Hyman G. Rickover

The problems facing most potential franchisees stem from a lack of understanding about the relationship between franchisor and franchisee. Buying a franchise is like buying a stream of income. A good rule of thumb is that the more reliable the stream of income, the more the franchise will cost, and the less control you'll have over your own business. Franchisors generally make their money by selling franchises, selling goods and services to those franchises, and receiving a percentage of revenues. The better franchises are those that make the lion's share of their profits through the franchisee's ongoing operations. That gives them a strong motivation to help you succeed. The better you do, they better they will do.

The franchisor rejected my application.

What's your problem?—This is an actual problem.

One problem at a time—This is also a single problem, whose solution is an appeal.

Focus on facts, not feelings—Don't dwell on anger and disappointment. Instead, focus on what you can do to turn the no around.

Become an expert—One reason for your rejection could have been your failure to become an expert on the financial needs and wants of the franchisor. Go back and check your research and fill in any gaps you uncover.

Create an environment of trust—Another reason for your rejection could have been your failure to get the franchisor to trust in your skills and abilities to run the business, or your capability to learn how to run the business. However, since franchisors make money selling franchises, and most offer training programs, odds are that if there's a lack of trust it's in your ability to raise the money, not manage the business.

Turn no into yes—As in every other appeal, the first step is to look behind the no and discover the reason for your rejection. In this instance it's likely the franchisor will readily provide you with the reason, since they're as eager to turn the no around as you are. Once you learn of the reason, search out new facts that will either refute it or make it moot. Perhaps you have a greater net worth than you showed on the application, since you failed to include the summer home your wife owns. Maybe you forgot to include that regular end-of-year bonus you receive from your employer, or to make note of some realistic financial expectations. Of you could have forgotten to clean up that mistake on your credit report resulting from a disputed credit card charge. Whatever the reason, provide some new facts and you're very likely to turn this rejection into an acceptance.

Will the franchisor do everything they said?

What's your problem?—This is a presenting problem. Your actual problem is that you haven't done a sufficient job becoming an expert on the franchisor's track record, financial health, and reputation.

One problem at a time—This is a single problem.

Focus on facts, not feelings—This problem is framed too subjectively. Don't accept general and ambiguous statements of reliability from the list of approved contacts provided by the franchisor. Instead, ask specific, factual questions. Did the franchisor provide the advertising campaign promised last year? Do deliveries arrive on time? How frequently are management refresher classes offered?

Become an expert—Clearly, the secret here is to become an expert on the experiences of other franchisees. Seek out all the franchisees in your region. Ask them specific questions about the promises made by the franchisor. Dig for potential problems. What would the franchisees change about the franchisor? Would they buy this franchise again?

Create an environment of trust—Express your thanks to other franchisees for their willingness to speak with you. Treat them as respected veterans of the business. Say that you admire their success and want to learn from their experience. Most businesspeople are happy to share their knowledge with noncompetitors, particularly those who share their enthusiasm for the industry.

Turn no into yes—Presumably there are at least hundreds of franchisees out there for you to speak with, so there should be no need to turn an individual refusal to speak with you around. If there are so few existing franchisees that it's essential you speak to each one, you're buying the wrong franchise. Remember: you're looking for a guaranteed stream of income, and that can only be documented by a substantial track record. In my opinion, it's better to start your own business than to buy into a fledgling franchise.

I'm afraid I'm going to end up working for them.

What's your problem?—This is a presenting problem. Your real problem is that you don't understand the nature of franchising. If you buy a franchise you will indeed be working for the "mother" company. A franchisee is a major, not a general. He has some control, but it's limited and subject to the orders of his superiors.

One problem at a time—This is a single problem.

Focus on facts, not feelings—Set aside your feelings about the relationship between a franchisor and a franchisee. Instead, focus on the facts: the text of the franchise agreement. That document will spell out exactly what you will and won't be able to control. If you can't accept the constraints the agreement places on your independence, you shouldn't buy the franchise.

Become an expert—You need to set aside your external research on franchising and this particular business, and instead conduct a thorough self-analysis. Do you really have the personality to be a franchisee? What do you really want from this business, or from any other business you run? Are you looking for an outlet for your creativity or are you looking for an income? Do you have trouble taking orders or conforming, or are you a good team player?

Create an environment of trust—You should trust the franchisor to stick to the terms of the agreement. You can count on them exerting as much control over you as the document allows. The real issue of trust in this problem is whether or not you trust your own self-analysis. There's too much time and money at stake here to delude yourself into thinking you'll be a happy franchisee when your personality is really that of an innovator. If you don't trust your own judgments bring in a team of problem mentors, individuals who've had both personal and professional experience with you, and ask their opinions.

Turn no into yes—There's no reason to appeal a thorough self-analysis.

Leasing Commercial Space

18

Shall I compare thee to a summer's day?
Thou art more lovely and more temperate.
Rough winds do shake the darling buds of May,
And summer's lease hath all too short a date.

William Shakespeare, Sonnet 18

Rent is one of the leading causes of business failures. On average, real estate represents between five and ten percent of a business's overhead—that's second only to labor. What makes this problematic is that almost every other expense can be reduced when business falls off. You can lay off excess staff. You can stop buying supplies and inventory. You can even cut off the telephone and utilities if you go out of business. But you can't stop paying the rent until your lease expires.

Of course, there are some ways around this problem. Savvy entrepreneurs try to avoid giving a personal guarantee to a landlord, or to sign the lease through a separate corporation specifically formed for just that purpose. Retaining the right to sublet gives you a chance to pass the cost along to another business. Unfortunately, commercial leases are so complex and arcane that it's rare for any entrepreneur to be able to crack their secrets. Even attorneys who don't specialize in commercial leases can be stymied by their complexity.

For all their intricacy, leases do have one thing going for them.

Whatever you think your problem with a commercial lease is, it's really this: it restricts your business's freedom to change.*

What if my business fails and I'm stuck with a long lease? (or) **What if I outgrow my space?** (or) **What if I'm making a mistake about this space?**

What's your problem?—Whatever you believe your problem to be it's really just a presenting problem for this: the lease restricts the ability of you and your business to change.

One problem at a time—Leases are a cluster of problems. Among the issues you'll need to address are: the term of the lease and any options to renew; who signs the document and is therefore legally responsible for rent payment; the accuracy of the lease's description of the space; pass-along charges; the assignability of the lease; the landlord's right to cancel for reasons other than nonpayment of rent; future rent increases; and occupancy date.

Focus on facts, not feelings—No lease is going to be perfect, since you and the landlord are at cross purposes. You want as much freedom and as little responsibility as possible under the agreement. The landlord wants you to be bound as tightly as possible. Rather than trying to "win," simply do the best you can to get the best deal you can, realizing that the better the space, the more constraints you may need to put up with. If you're in a business in which location is important, you may need to put up with quite a few restraints to get the kind of space you need to be successful.

Become an expert—The real heavy lifting here should be done by your attorney. However, you still need to know about the issues involved so you can make informed decisions in your discussions with your lawyer.

Short-term leases put you at the landlord's mercy. If you start to do well, he'll hold you up for more rent. Long-term leases carry the risk of outliving your business. The solution is often to get a short-term lease with options to renew at affordable rent increases that extend at least as far as your anticipated break-even point, if you're a start-up.

---

*I'm serious. I can't think of any problem with a commercial lease that isn't really just another way of saying that it restricts either you or your business's ability to change in one way or another, for whatever reason. I've listed three commercial lease problems clients most often bring to me. Feel free to substitute your own problem for one of those, if necessary.

The rent increases should be described fully, both in terms of amount and timing.

Your lease should be signed by a corporation, not an individual. Even though you're sure your business will continue to succeed, you must insulate yourself from any personal liability if it fails.

Make sure the lease accurately reflects the square footage of your space. Pay only for "carpetable" space.

Make sure the building's "pass alongs"—the charges for such things as public areas, air-conditioning, heating, taxes, and insurance—don't add up to more than 100 percent of the costs.

Try to get a lease that's assignable or at least that lets you sublet for "any legal use" or for "general use" by a business similar to your own. Remember that a retailer without an assignable lease can't sell his business.

Examine any rights the landlord has to cancel the lease for reasons other than your breach of the agreement. Make sure there are specific reasons given for cancellation and you'll receive adequate compensation based on future values and loss of income.

Finally, an occupancy date should be provided. If the space isn't delivered "vacant" as promised by that date, then you should have the right to terminate the agreement.

Create an environment of trust—The more you can get a landlord to trust you and your business, the more luck you'll have in negotiating an advantageous, or at least fair, lease. Commercial landlords are really partners in their tenants' businesses. When a tenant does well, the landlord does well. And, when a tenant fails, the landlord needs to find another tenant. If you can get your landlord excited about your future, he's apt to give you enough breathing space to grow. If, on the other hand, the landlord doesn't have confidence in your future, he'll try to squeeze as much out of you as he can, as quickly as he can.

Turn no into yes—There really isn't an appeal in this process, since it's a cluster of related issues rather than a single problem. The solution comes through a give-and-take negotiation between your attorney and the landlord's attorney, with you and the landlord behind the scenes pulling the strings. There should be no real winner or loser. The more desirable the space, the more restrictions on your freedom you'll have to accept. And alternatively, the more desirable you are as a tenant, the more freedoms the landlord will need to allow.

Professionals 19

A lawyer with his briefcase can steal more than a hundred men with guns.

Mario Puzo, The Godfather

Every potential problem with a professional can be resolved ahead of time if you go about the hiring process correctly. Only hire professionals on recommendation. These leads can come from other professionals on your team (your lawyer recommending an accountant), from family or friends whose judgment you trust and who are at a similar economic level, or, if you have no other option, from a professional organization. If, for example, you've no other way to find an attorney, contact the local bar association, explain what your needs are, and ask them to recommend some candidates.

Notice I write *candidates*, not *candidate*. You want to be able to pick and choose from at least two or three potential professionals. Interview each candidate at their place of business, and ask them about their experience, expertise, procedures, and fees. If a candidate is "too busy" to hold this interview without charge, scratch his name off your list.

Once you've chosen from among your candidates, memorialize your relationship with an engagement letter that spells out the rights and responsibilities of both parties. Most important of all, the engagement letter should explain how the relationship will be ended, if necessary.

Unfortunately, most people don't follow these simple rules when hiring professionals. As a result, they can end up facing some obstacles that are very difficult to overcome.

She won't represent me.

What's your problem?—This is a real problem. For instance, if you are facing a full-scale IRS audit, you want the best tax lawyer in town on your side. If she turns you down, and there's a big drop-off in skill between her and the second best tax lawyer, you are in dire straits.

One problem at a time—This is a single problem.

Focus on facts, not feelings—Don't let feelings of personal rejection enter into the equation. This is a business decision on the part of the professional. Respond in a businesslike manner rather than emotionally and you'll have a better chance of succeeding.

Become an expert—You need to know how much the professional generally earns from situations like yours, and how that compares to the industry average. In addition, you should have an idea of how long and how difficult your case might be. Finally, it helps to know all you can about the personal as well as business background of the professional in question. Any personal connection you can uncover can help generate trust.

Create an environment of trust—While normally it's up to the professional to generate trust in the client, in the case of highly sought after individuals the roles are often reversed. You don't want to come to the professional as a supplicant, but you do want to create as much of a bond as possible, and to at least get her to respect your integrity and candor.

Turn no into yes—Ask why the professional turned you down. There are really only two reasons you'll be given: either she didn't think your matter had the potential to offer her sufficient money, or she believes there's a conflict of interest.

If she doesn't see your account as being profitable enough, you need to offer new facts that change her initial judgment. For instance, perhaps she didn't realize you intended her to handle other matters for you in future, or didn't know that your business has been growing fifty percent a year for the past three years in a row. Maybe she didn't realize that, as president of the Lions Club and membership secretary of your national trade association, you could be a source of other clients for her. Present yourself as more of a profit center than you first appear and you'll turn her no around.

If she believes representing you might be a conflict of interest you need to investigate the matter. Ask her about the current client who she believes is a competitor of yours. Don't appeal the decision if she's correct in her analysis. Simply thank her for her integrity and ask her to recommend the second best professional in town. However, if her analysis isn't accurate, feel free to ask for a reconsideration. Point out how you're not a direct competitor of the other client, explaining the key differences between your businesses, and show how representing you wouldn't at all be a conflict of interest. If you make a rational case you'll turn her no around.

Do I have to tell her everything?

What's your problem?—This is a real problem in dealing with every professional other than a lawyer. Because of the nature of the attorney/client privilege, you can tell your lawyer anything without fear that it will ever be divulged. Other professionals aren't bound by as strict a code of conduct.

One problem at a time—This is a single problem.

Focus on facts, not feelings—The trouble with this problem is that it is framed far too broadly and, as a result, becomes an emotional issue. Put it in more specific terms: do you have to tell her everything that pertains to the matter she's working on.

Become an expert—If you're afraid of telling your professional everything she needs to know in order to do her job, then you haven't done a good enough job of becoming an expert during your hiring of her. You need to go back and review the information you gathered at that point. If it's still not enough to convince you to divulge all the information necessary then you've hired the wrong person.

Create an environment of trust—If she hasn't generated enough trust in you to tell her everything she needs to know to do the job, then you should find another professional.

Turn no into yes—You've no appeal to this problem . . . although the professional may try to appeal your decision to fire her.

I'm afraid to fire her.

What's your problem?—This is a presenting problem that often hides a very tough actual problem. What accounts for the fear of firing a professional is that they can be a repository of important information and documents pertaining to your personal or business life. The fear that they know more about your situation than anyone else could ever learn is simply a cover for your embarrassment or anxiety at terminating someone who has worked with you for a long time. However, the fear that if you fire a professional she may hold on to your documents, making your life and your next professional's job a lot more difficult, is quite real. Your problem isn't so much the firing, but how to get your documents out of the hands of a professional that you've fired.

One problem at a time—This is a single problem.

Focus on facts, not feelings—Forget about feelings of anger or resentment or discomfort. Focus instead on the facts: the professional has your papers and you need to get them back. You need to do whatever it takes to get those documents back.

Become an expert—Learn all you can about mediation and dispute resolution programs offered by the professional's national association. Speak with others about the procedure for getting back your documents. If the professional makes a claim against you for unpaid fees, investigate the validity of her claim.

Create an environment of trust—It is difficult to recreate trust in a professional relationship after you've fired someone. Instead, work on creating trust with any third parties who may be mediating the problem.

Turn no into yes—When a professional refuses to return your documents you must ask why. If you're told it's because you still owe some unpaid fees, there's little you can do to turn the no around other than pay the funds owed. In many states professionals can place a lien on your property until they're paid. If it seems that the delay in turning over your documents is simply spite, ask them to reconsider, before you turn the case over to their professional association. Should that threat not be sufficient to get them to return your papers, make it clear you will make a nuisance of yourself until they hand over your property.

I don't know if I can trust her (or) **I don't know if she's competent.**

What's your problem?—These are always presenting problems. The real problem is that you didn't do an adequate job during the hiring process. All your fears about trust and competence should have been resolved before you hired her.

One problem at a time—This is actually a series of problems. You didn't get recommendations. You didn't develop a field of candidates. You didn't interview each candidate. You didn't check their references. And you didn't get an engagement letter. The way to solve them is to turn back the clock and address them in order.

Focus on facts, not feelings—Don't worry about embarrassment. Focus instead on the fact that you need to go about a rehiring process in a systematic rational manner.

Become an expert—You now need to follow all the steps of becoming an expert that you didn't follow when you first hired this professional. Get your recommendations, conduct interviews, check references, and draft an engagement letter.

Create an environment of trust—You also now need to develop the environment of trust that wasn't there previously. That can only be achieved through a candid discussion about your needs and wants and the professional's ability to help you achieve them.

Turn no into yes—The appeal process in this problem is a bit unusual. Since you've already hired the professional, you need to set up some kind of rehiring process. My suggestion is to cast the situation as part of your annual (or semiannual) personnel review process. Explain that every year (or every couple of years) you ask each and every member of your staff, as well as all your professionals, to tender their resignations. At that point you go through the process of rehiring each and every one of them. If, upon review, you're not happy with any of them, you accept their resignation. Having established the procedure, then go about hiring the professional in the proper manner by putting her name at the top of your list of candidates. If in this rehiring process you don't overcome your fears about her competence or trustworthiness, accept her resignation and hire someone else.

Hiring Employees

20

The best-looking résumé may come from the candidate who hires the best résumé writer or from the candidate who simply has the most experience writing résumés.

Robert Half

I have to admit, I've never been nominated for the boss-of-the-year award. I expect a lot from my employees and believe an office is a place of business, not a home away from home. That being said, I've never had any trouble hiring people. Why? Because I always pay fair market value and I'm clear about my goals and expectations. I'd humbly suggest that if you adopt an approach to hiring similar to mine you might also avoid hiring problems.

My staff works hard because I try not to have any more people on the payroll than I need. Because I run such a tight ship I look for people who are flexible and adaptable. If I need a specialist for a period of time I hire a temp or consultant. The characteristics I most value, in addition to flexibility, are predictability and candor. I'd rather have a person who consistently does B work, than someone who sometimes does A work but other times falls down to C work. Predictability allows me to compensate in advance for any failings so I know all the bases will be covered. I'd also rather have someone who admits he doesn't know something, or has made a mistake, than someone who tries to wing it or cover up an error. I'm not looking for my staff to be superstars . . . that's my job. I just want them to work hard, do their best, and be honest with me. I plan on staffers staying with me for anywhere from one to three years. Shorter than that and a temp would be more economical. Longer than that and it would be more profitable to outsource the job.

He turned down my offer.

What's your problem?—If you found only one candidate who was head and shoulders above the rest, and he turned your job offer down, then this is a real problem. Otherwise it's just a mask for annoyance at someone rejecting you.

One problem at a time—This is a single problem.

Focus on facts, not feelings—Rephrase this problem so you don't act as if it's a rejection of you. This isn't about you, it's about him, the job description, or the salary.

Become an expert—Go back and double-check your earlier research into the market value for the position. Make sure that you weren't lowballing the salary. Similarly, reanalyze the job profile. Are you expecting too much?

Create an environment of trust—Consider whether you did anything during the interview process to make the candidate uncomfortable or angry. While it's not your role as an interviewer to get the candidates to trust you, making them restive won't help you attract quality people.

Turn no into yes—Like all appeals, this one begins by discerning the reason for the no. Contact the candidate and express surprise at his rejection. Explain that you were very impressed by him, are disappointed by his decision, and would be grateful for some feedback about the process. Don't be a supplicant. Instead ask him what the motivating factors were for his decision, so you can have a better idea of what future candidates will think.

If he says you weren't offering enough salary, say that you have an honest disagreement about market value. Note that all you can do is promise to pay more as the market increases. If that's not sufficient, wish him well. You cannot start paying more than market value for people or there will be no limit to your payroll.

If he says there was something troubling about the job description, solicit details and see if you can reach some kind of compromise. For instance, if he objects to the travel demands, explain that perhaps he misunderstood, and note that much of the client contact can be done through teleconferencing instead.

I can't find anyone good.

What's your problem?—This is a presenting problem. Your actual problem is that either you're not offering sufficient compensation, or you're expecting too much from the position.

One problem at a time—This is a single problem.

Focus on facts, not feelings—What you *want* to pay someone, or how much work you *want* to get from them, doesn't matter. This isn't about your wants, or even the candidates' wants, it's about the labor market. If receptionists are being paid at least $20,000 a year, that's what you'll need to pay. If they don't have the time to do any more than light filing while doing their receptionist duties, then you can't expect them also to reorganize and digitize your records.

Become an expert—Check with headhunters, employment agencies, your industry association, the editor of your trade journal, and the local chamber of commerce to learn exactly what the market rate and traditional job profile are for the kind of position you're filling.

Create an environment of trust—By offering less than market value, and simultaneously having unrealistic expectations, you're certainly not creating an environment of trust. Actually, you're frightening people off. You don't need to become Mr. Rogers. You just need to have realistic expectations and offer fair value.

Turn no into yes—There's no point in going back to the poor candidates who were desperate enough to respond to your initial offer. Why give an unattractive candidate a second chance?

I don't know if I believe what he says.

What's your problem?—This is also a presenting problem. You're actually answering your own question. If you say you don't know whether or not to believe a candidate, you're really saying you don't believe them.

One problem at a time—This is a single problem.

Focus on facts, not feelings—Don't feel bad about distrusting a candidate. It was their role to create trust in you, and they failed. It's not your fault, it's theirs.

Become an expert—Sure, you can try to check a candidate's references, investigate his background, and determine his expertise. But if you have a gut feeling and simply don't believe him, there's no point in wasting any more time.

Create an environment of trust—They didn't create an environment of trust, so you needn't bother anymore.

Turn no into yes—It's up to the candidate, not you, to try to turn this no around. That being said, if for some reason, despite my advice, you feel the need to give this person a try, make it clear there will need to be a trial or probationary period of, say, three months. If they work out, fine. If they don't, they'll be fired without receiving any severance.

He wants a contract.

What's your problem?—This is a real problem, since more and more employees are realizing employment contracts are essential in today's chaotic job market.

One problem at a time—This is a single problem.

Focus on facts, not feelings—You need to frame your problem a bit more narrowly in order to solve it. Just wanting a contract isn't really a problem, since a contract can say as much or as little as you'd like. It's only a problem if the employee wants a contract that restricts your freedoms, either by guaranteeing him a certain term of employment and/or specified salary increases.

Become an expert—You need to become an expert on the wide variety of things that can be part of a contract. For example, just because there's an employment contract doesn't mean the employee isn't still employed "at will." The contract can specifically say employment is at will. It can simply be a formal statement of the terms of the at will employment. The contract could describe the job, state the salary, outline the benefits, and even explore severance pay, just as long as it doesn't say how long the employee will be working for you, and what his future salary increases will be. You could even turn the employee's request for a contract to your advantage by inserting a clause that temporarily keeps the employee from working for a competitor if they leave or are terminated.

Create an environment of trust—You'll create a tremendous level of trust between you and a job candidate if you don't immediately rule out the idea of an employment contract. Often, all a candidate is looking for is a written guarantee of what is being offered verbally. Even savvy candidates might be satisfied with just negotiating a severance package, in exchange for a no compete clause.

Turn no into yes—Because an employment contract can contain whatever you want, there's no need for you to immediately say no when a candidate asks for one. Rather than the candidate appealing your no, or your appealing their turning down your job offer, the two of you can simply negotiate the terms of an agreement that's mutually satisfying.

Firing Employees

21

Severities should be dealt out all at once, that by their sudden-
ness they may give less offense; benefits should be handed out
drop by drop, that they be relished the more.

Niccolo Machiavelli

Machiavelli is absolutely correct. When you terminate someone it
should be done as quickly and cleanly as possible. You want to be a
human executioner, not a torturer who prolongs the employee's agony.
That requires obsessive planning, scripted dialogue, and almost ritual-
ized behavior. Offer sympathy, but not hope of a reconsideration. The
termination act should be as swift and clean as a guillotine. Severance
payments, however, are another story.

Most of the fears that employers have about terminating someone
arise because they fail to realize that severance is, to use the great Flo-
rentine statesman's words, a benefit, not a severity. In most of the
United States, a terminated employee does not have an automatic legal
right to severance. It has, however, become an accepted practice in
cases when an employee has been fired without cause. Your fears can
be cured simply by making severance a process, rather than a one-time
payment. Instead of handing a terminated employee a check and
showing them the door, link the initial and continued payment of severance to the behavior you desire.

I'm afraid I'll break the law.

What's your problem?—This is an all too real problem today.

One problem at a time—This is a single, but very dangerous, problem.

Focus on facts, not feelings—You're being entirely rational in having this fear. Because of the, I believe, justifiable proliferation of protective statutes, there has been a resulting increase in the number of claims of illegal terminations.

Become an expert—Expertise is essential in terminating someone without being held legally liable. However, most of the expertise you need can be hired. What you need to learn is who is and isn't a "protected" minority. Terminations can be considered discriminatory if they were made on the basis of age, gender, disability, sexual orientation, race, religion, national origin, or even marital status. If you plan to terminate anyone who *might* fall under one of these categories, then you need to speak with a termination expert—either a human resources consultant, an outplacement counselor, or an employment lawyer. The expert will then help you establish a foolproof termination process that should protect you from legal liability.

Create an environment of trust—In this scenario, you need to have developed trust in your professional.

Turn no into yes—As long as you have followed the pattern laid out by your expert you should need to deal with any appeal, or threat, from the employee. However, if you're afraid of a nuisance lawsuit, you might consider treating the threat as just an effort to increase the severance package. In all honesty, that's how I advise using this leverage whenever I represent an employee who may have been unfairly terminated. Obviously, you should never retract the termination. But if it makes your life easier, increasing the severance might be justified in the circumstances.

They'll ask for more severance.

What's your problem?—This is a real problem, albeit rare. Few people actually ask for more severance . . . unless they're a client or reader of mine.

One problem at a time—This is a cluster of problems, taking the shape of a single problem. Instead of looking at cash as the only element of a severance package, you can actually make the problem easier to solve by focusing on the various other items that could be offered. Continued health coverage can be discussed. Use of the office and its facilities as a job-hunting base can be debated. Ownership of office equipment—like a laptop or cell phone—can be negotiated. References can be made part of the package. The more issues brought into play the easier it will be to come up with a compromise solution.

Focus on facts, not feelings—Don't get angry at the request. Focus instead on the facts. You want the employee to leave quickly without damaging your business. The employee also wants to leave quickly, but with as much of a cushion against financial ruin as they can get. When push comes to shove it's really just a negotiation over what you're willing to "pay" for their speedy and cooperative departure.

Become an expert—It helps if you have some expertise on the current state of the job market. That way you'll be able to differentiate between rational pleas for help and unjustified blackmail.

Create an environment of trust—Let's face it: whatever professional trust existed between you and this employee dissolved when you terminated them.

Turn no into yes—Since you aren't legally required to pay any severance, you can always resort to a take-it-or-leave-it position. However, I'd suggest you temper that somewhat by giving them two or three weeks to consider your take-it-or-leave-it offer, during which time they must continue to go about the basics of their job. In effect you're saying you'll give them another two or three weeks' pay in exchange for their doing some minimal work and then leaving with the original severance offer.

They'll sabotage my business (or) They'll go after my customers (or) They'll bad-mouth me.

What's your problem?—Unless you're feeling guilty over firing someone, these are all real problems.

One problem at a time—They are also all single problems.

Focus on facts, not feelings—However, none of them are rational if you act prudently.

Become an expert—The key information to absorb is that severance isn't an entitlement and need not be a one-time payment. Put together a severance package that is a process contingent on the behavior you desire. For instance, offer to pay the two months' severance out in weekly installments, as long as the employee refrains from disrupting your business or speaking with your customers. Or tie acceptance of the severance package with acceptance of an agreement not to unfairly compete.

Create an environment of trust—After a termination there's no longer any trust between an employer or employee. Whatever agreements you have must be in writing.

Turn no into yes—There's no need for an appeal here. If the employee refuses to agree not to disrupt your business, or to refrain from speaking to your customers, simply take your severance offer off the table and show them the door.

Suppliers

22

Thrust ivrybody, but cut th' ca-ards.

Finley Peter Dunne, Casual Observations

The more you and your suppliers act like partners, the fewer problems you'll have. However, in order to act like partners you'll need to be well suited to each other. Partnerships, whether between individuals or companies, require that the whole—the partnership—equals more than just the sum of the parts. The best partnerships are those in which the partners complement each other, providing skills, traits, and abilities the other lacks.

The classic example of this symbiotic relationship is a retail partnership between an "inside person"—who focuses on the bookkeeping, management, and buying—and an "outside person"—who concentrates on the sales, marketing, and promotion. The equivalent example of a business/supplier partnership is a small, bare-bones, entrepreneurial business that focuses on its core operation, which teams up with a large, full-service supplier, which provides every kind of customer service under the sun. Such a relationship will work wonderfully because the supplier offers exactly what the entrepreneur needs, while the entrepreneur provides the one thing the supplier lacks, an outlet to sell their products to consumers. The more your relationships with your suppliers fit this partnership model, the fewer problems you'll have.

I don't think I'm getting the best deal.

What's your problem?—This is a real problem. If you could get a better deal, either from this supplier or another supplier, than you're, in effect, losing money.

One problem at a time—This is actually a cluster of problems. A better deal not only involves price but also terms, promotional help, and marketing allowances as well.

Focus on facts, not feelings—Don't focus on the fact that you've been personally cheated. Instead, concentrate on your getting a lower price, better terms, more promotional help, or a larger marketing allowance. The idea is not to worry about the fact that you're being shortchanged, but to fixate on the actual amounts involved. That way you'll keep from becoming emotional.

Become an expert—There are two ways to determine whether or not you're getting the best deal possible. First, you can speak with your competitors or third parties who have knowledge about your competitors' operations. Second, and preferably, you can go out and solicit better offers from other suppliers.

Create an environment of trust—Don't jump to the conclusion that your supplier is knowingly shortchanging you. The individuals you work with may not know of special deals that have been worked out with other businesses. Similarly, your supplier may have no idea of what kind of deals its own competitors are offering. Because you may be bringing them "news," it's important that you provide them with as much documentation as possible so they trust your numbers. That's difficult in the case of inside information you've gathered about a competitor's operation. However, you should be able to provide enough detail so they can conduct an internal investigation. In the case of a better offer from another supplier, you'll need to show them some written documentation.

Turn no into yes—There's really no need to launch an appeal here. If a supplier can improve your deal in one way or another without losing money, it will. That's capitalism. If the supplier can't, find another supplier who can.

I'm afraid they'll drop me.

What's your problem?—If you're dealing with a "star" supplier this is a real problem. There are some suppliers who have so much leverage in an industry that they're not above pulling their product line from one business if they're unhappy with it for some reason or another.

One problem at a time—This is a single problem.

Focus on facts, not feelings—If there's some sign the supplier is unhappy with you, this is a rational fear. If there's no sign of unhappiness, or if the supplier doesn't have the power to pick and choose among businesses, you're just being paranoid.

Become an expert—If you're an expert on the needs and wants of your supplier then you'll have a sense whether or not they're happy with you. If you don't already have that expertise, start acquiring it as soon as you sense there could be something amiss. Then, develop a memo outlining all the things you will do to repair your relationship. Just keep your fingers crossed that you still have time to act.

Create an environment of trust—Having researched your supplier's needs and wants, and having uncovered that you're not meeting them, you need to work hard to reestablish trust. Using all the trust-building techniques you can muster, make it clear to your supplier that you value them as a partner and are willing to do whatever it takes to make that partnership mutually profitable.

Turn no into yes—In this case, the entire process is an appeal, whether you've actually been dropped or not. Even if you just have a hint of trouble, or hear a rumor, you must react with the same urgency as if you'd been dropped. The new facts you're offering as grounds for reconsideration are your new knowledge and understanding of what the supplier needs, and your redoubled efforts to make sure the relationship works.

A competitor of mine is getting special treatment.

What's your problem?—This is a real problem. Anytime a competitor is getting an unfair advantage will impact your bottom line.

One problem at a time—This is a single problem if there's only one type of special treatment—say they're being allowed to return goods with alacrity. However it's a cluster if they're being offered a number of different types of special treatment.

Focus on facts, not feelings—The key here is not to get angry, but to get even. Recriminations are irrational. You simply want equal treatment.

Become an expert—The difficulty here is that your information probably comes from an inside source who needs anonymity, or from someone who has heard a rumor but has no facts to base it on. Clearly, your competitor won't come clean. Still, despite the sketchy nature of your information, all you need to do in this type of situation is plant the seed. If it's true, you won't be asked for documentation of a shady deal.

Create an environment of trust—Express your disappointment. Say that you thought you had developed a relationship of trust with the supplier but have heard rumors that your competitors are receiving a special deal. Treat this not as a business problem but as a personal affront, and you'll get a quick response.

Turn no into yes—Either the supplier will be embarrassed and admit the situation is true, or they will deny it. If it's true they will either promise to end the practice or extend it to you as well. If they deny it, they're likely telling the truth, since they don't know how much information you actually have, and being caught in two lies would spell the end of your business relationship. In either case there's no reason to appeal.

Clients and Customers

23

Le client n'a jamais tort.
The customer is never wrong.

César Ritz

Landing a client or customer is one of the most difficult tasks facing any businessperson. Unfortunately, keeping that client or customer is even tougher. That's because you can't control all the factors influencing customer and client decisions. You can do an excellent job for a customer, but if someone else opens up shop ten minutes closer to the customer's home or business, you can lose him. You may have created an incredible bond of trust with a client, but if someone else offers to provide the same service for less money you can lose her. You can do a great job, have wonderful rapport, and provide a terrific value, all in a convenient location, and yet lose the business because the client, or even her spouse, thinks it's better to spend those funds in another manner. All you can do is your best . . . and remain an expert in the needs of your clients or customers.

It's this search for constant expertise that serves as the solution to forestalling every common customer or client problem. Keep asking your clients how they feel about the service you're providing. Solicit constant feedback from customers. A suggestion box isn't sufficient. Regularly ask all of them if they are happy, if there is anything further you can do for them, of if there is anything you can do to make your product or service better. This can't just be a facade of concern; it must be a real effort to nip any snags or qualms in the bud before they blossom into full problems.

Once a problem with a customer or client has developed, whatever it is, you'll need to treat it in the same manner: as an appeal for a reconsideration, based on new facts. The underlying no in every one of these situations is that the client or customer is in some way unhappy. The specific problem is just the immediate manifestation of that unhappiness. You need to find out what is wrong and offer to cure it.

They won't hire me (or) They've fired me.

What's your problem?—When a customer or client chooses not to buy your product or service, or to stop buying, it's a real problem. In fact, it's about as real a problem as you can have. Without customers or clients your business will die.

One problem at a time—If you're addressing the fact that one particular customer or client won't or will no longer do business with you, then this is probably a single problem involving the reason for the refusal. However, if you've run into a regular pattern of customer or client refusals and terminations then you're apt to be facing a cluster of problems: all the reasons for the refusals.

Focus on facts, not feelings—In order to solve this problem you must move beyond the feeling that you've been rejected and focus instead on why you've been turned down or fired. Framing the problem in a general manner won't do you any good. Instead you must sharpen your description of the problem. You need to focus on why they won't hire you or why they've chosen to fire you.

Become an expert—Obviously, the basis for this appeal is becoming an expert on the client's or customer's dissatisfaction.

Create an environment of trust—If you haven't already created an environment of trust with this customer or client, you now need to double your efforts in order to get the true reason behind their no. Humbly ask them for help in improving your business. Beseech them to tell you whatever it was that turned them off. Bring up the most sensitive possibilities yourself—such as garb, grooming, or pricing.

Turn no into yes—Whatever reason you're given for the no, express your thanks for the response. If it was a personal failing, offer apologies, and ask the client or customer to reconsider, based on your assurance that such behavior will never happen again. If the reason for the rejection is an area where you have some latitude—maybe you can do the work speedier than you'd originally promised—again ask for a reconsideration based on changing facts. Many times, customers and clients are so flattered by the importance with which you now so obviously hold them, and the dedicated customer service you're demonstrating, that they quickly turn their no into a yes. However, if their no is based on something you cannot change—perhaps your hourly fee—simply express thanks for their honesty, and acceptance of their decision.

They won't pay me.

What's your problem?—This is a real problem, even more destructive than not being hired or being fired. When a customer or client chooses not to use your service or buy your product, you've only lost the investment you made in soliciting their business, and potential revenues. When a customer or client chooses not to pay you for work you've already done or a product you've already provided, the funds are coming right out of your pocket.

One problem at a time—Whether it's one client who's refusing to pay or a group of customers who are slow in paying, this is almost always a single problem. Either it's a problem unique to the sole rejecter, or a single poor procedure or policy being taken advantage of by a handful of customers.

Focus on facts, not feelings—Just as in not being hired, or being fired, in order to solve this problem you'll need to focus on why the customer or client isn't paying.

Become an expert—In order to solve this problem you need to become an expert on your customer's business as well as your own. That's because the problem might not be caused by you at all. The customer's business may be undercapitalized. Or the client may just be taking advantage of your good nature and relaxed terms. Perhaps he's decided not to pay for a while to "see what happens."

Create an environment of trust—In order to solve this problem without losing the client or customer, you need to walk a very careful path. If you're too aggressive and demonstrate that you've lost trust in the other party, you'll not only lose future business from them, but you'll probably also have a hard time collecting what you're already owed. If you don't bring the issue up at all, it won't get solved.

Turn no into yes—The secret here is to try to frame the issue as if it's really about you. Ask if there is something you're doing to make it difficult for them to pay on time. Perhaps you can change the date they're usually billed, or perhaps you should bill them twice a month rather than just once.

Clients or customers who have simply been taking advantage of you will often latch onto one of your suggestions as a way to save face. Having been called on their bad behavior, however nicely, they'll now toe the line.

Clients who have been having problems of their own will generally be prodded into a confession by your concerns. If a client tells you the reason she's paying slowly is that her own business is having problems, offer to help. Suggest she speak with your accountant. Offer the name of your banker. Most times, by bringing the issue up and offering to help you'll at least move your bill to the top of the pile.

If neither of these techniques works you'll simply have to inform the client or customer that you'll be charging them interest on their outstanding bills. And even if it means losing a customer, at some point you'll need to stop doing business with someone who hasn't paid. If you aren't able to turn their not paying around, then they're not worth keeping as a customer.

Vendors

24

Do not persist in folly. Some make it a duty of failure and having started down the wrong road, think it is a badge of character to continue.

Baltasar Gracián y Morales

If you want to avoid problems with your vendors, make sure you're very important to them, more important than the amount of your bill might indicate. A vendor to whom you're just another customer, or just another dollar, is a vendor who won't deliver on time or provide what they promised.

So how do you become more than just an invoice? One way is to spread the word that you're looking for a vendor and solicit bids. Rather than looking for vendors on your own, publicize that you're searching and you'll get bids from vendors who are hungry for your business. You will be more important to someone who actively wants your business than you will be to someone you had to ask to accept your money.

Once you have a number of vendors pursuing your business, look for those who have a special reason to value you as a customer. Perhaps they want to crack into your industry. Maybe they'd like the exposure you'll provide them. They might be desperate for a more consistent, if not sizable, stream of revenues. Or it could be that you're offering them an opportunity to use new or very profitable types of services. Be more than just a paycheck and you'll never need to worry about their delivering on their promises.

What if they're not reliable? (or) **What if their product isn't good?** (or) **What if they don't deliver on time?**

What's your problem?—While all these fears are legitimate, they're also all covers for other problems. Your real problem is that you don't trust the vendor because you didn't do an adequate job of investigating him before you hired him. It doesn't matter whether the problem is extant—he's already fallen behind—or expectant—you're afraid he will fall behind. The problem is you simply don't trust the vendor to do the job.

One problem at a time—This is, in all likelihood, a cluster of problems. You're not only worried, say, about the vendor delivering on time, you're also probably worried about the quality of his product. Then, if you've made a promise based on the vendor's promise, you're also worried about your delivering on time as well, and how your own customer will respond if you can't. Basically, you have no confidence in anything about the vendor, and are worried about how the vendor's failings will impact every aspect of your business.

Focus on facts, not feelings—Rather than giving in to your worst fears and focusing on the possibility of total failure, concentrate on the current facts. Is the vendor still on schedule? Have you been regularly checking the quality of his work? What are the specific problems that exist right now? If you find the vendor is on schedule, and your spot checks reveal quality work, your general fear of failure is irrational. Keep your fingers crossed and start looking for someone else in whom you'll have confidence. On the other hand, if you find problems with the schedule or quality you now have something concrete to work on.

Become an expert—If you had done a thorough job of investigating this vendor you wouldn't be in this mess. But, rather than dwelling on that, do your best to now become an expert in the vendor's business. Your goal is to help him find ways to get back on schedule and to improve his work, or to stick to a schedule and provide a quality product.

Whichever is the case, start looking for replacement vendors, and this time, do a thorough research job. Since obviously you're not comfortable with this vendor, you'll need a replacement sooner or later. Hopefully your newfound expertise will help you get out of the current mess. If not, you want to be able to jump to another vendor as soon as possible.

Create an environment of trust—This vendor failed to create an environment of trust in his relationship with you. Don't let anything he does from this point on cloud your decision to switch to another vendor. At this point you've no need to get him to trust you. In fact, you'll probably do better getting him to fear you a little bit. You can do that by being very direct and businesslike in manner, and extremely punctual in seeking feedback. For instance, call every afternoon at 3 P.M. to check on the schedule, get your status report, and then end the dialogue. Don't engage in any friendly banter.

Turn no into yes—There really is no appeal to this problem. You certainly should not give the vendor another chance: there are too many other reliable vendors out there who want your business enough to do a good and timely job.

They won't do work for me.

What's your problem?—If this vendor is the only one in the world who can deliver what you need, then this is an actual problem, whether they've already actually said no, or you're just afraid they'll turn you down. But if this isn't the Picasso of vendors, it's a presenting problem. Your real problem is that you've so little confidence in your own and your business's abilities that you think your success depends on a vendor and that you won't be worth that vendor's interest.

One problem at a time—Whether rational or not, expectant or extant, this is a single problem.

Focus on facts, not feelings—If this is an extant problem—they've in fact turned you down—set aside feelings of rejection and instead concentrate on why they won't work for you. If this is an expectant problem look closely at the specific factors that can have influenced their decision.

Become an expert—This entire problem is actually an appeal, whether it's to a real or an anticipated rejection. The most important information you need to find out is why they have, or would, you suspect, turn you down. If they've already rejected you, ask them for the reason. If you're anticipating rejection, speak with others in the industry and find out all you can about the vendor's needs and wants.

Create an environment of trust—Trust really isn't an issue in solving this problem. If this vendor is truly unique, and so above the norm in terms of quality, odds are his reputation alone is enough to create trust in his customers. If you try to create trust in the vendor you'll come off as desperate. In that case he might pity you, but he won't work for you.

Turn no into yes—If the vendor turns you down because he "doesn't have the time," or doesn't find your project "interesting," don't bother appealing. No matter how good he is you shouldn't settle for anything less than a full commitment. Instead, ask him to recommend the "second best" vendor in the business. That request alone may get him to change his mind.

If he rejects you because he doesn't believe you'll offer him enough profit, appeal based on your ability to bring him other business through referrals, or to provide him with entry into a new field.

Marketing 25

The meek have to inherit the earth—they sure don't know how to market it.

Jeno F. Palucci

I never ceased to be amazed at how little most small-business people know about marketing. Every single marketing problem I've ever helped a client deal with is the result of misunderstanding.

The most common misperception I confront among my clients is that, due to the special nature of their business, they don't need to do any marketing. On the contrary, every business needs to do marketing. And, in fact, the more specialized your business, the more marketing you probably need to do. My clients who are professionals and service providers are the worst offenders in this regard. They mistakenly equate marketing with advertising, and then denounce it as beneath their dignity. I try to explain that there's far more to marketing than advertising. I offer suggestions on publicity and public relations. I discuss newsletters and Web pages. I talk about teaching classes and giving speeches. I explain how to write and place newspaper articles and generate positive word of mouth. I offer advice about choosing office stationery and taping the right answering machine message. I even discuss how pricing can be an element of marketing. My message is always, in essence, the same: marketing is the cultivation and spreading of a positive image that will attract and, by reinforcement, keep clients and customers. As such, it is a sine qua non for any business.

Won't it cost a fortune?

What's your problem?—Your real problem is you don't understand the nature of marketing: it doesn't necessarily cost a great deal of money.

One problem at a time—This is single problem.

Focus on facts, not feelings—You are viewing marketing emotionally, rather than rationally. Marketing, while an expense, is intended to generate increased revenues by exposing your products or services to a larger market of potential clients or customers. The issue you should be concentrating on isn't how much marketing will cost, but how much you need to spend and where, in order to increase your revenues enough to generate a profit.

Become an expert—Become a student of marketing. Look for contacts within your industry or professional organization for advice on marketing. Contact your local chamber of commerce. Investigate courses at the local college. Speak with other successful practitioners or businesspeople in your profession or business. Talk to public relations and advertising agencies. Ask the sales representatives of local media outlets—newspapers, magazines, radio stations, cable television stations—to provide you with information on the reach of their particular medium.

Create an environment of trust—Trust isn't an issue here. You can solve your problem by defining your situation rationally and then becoming an expert.

Turn no into yes—There isn't a need for an appeal, since the no is inside your own head.

I'm not good with strangers.

What's your problem?—Your real problem is you don't understand the nature of marketing: it doesn't necessarily require you to become a media personality or to personally interact with others.

One problem at a time—This is single problem.

Focus on facts, not feelings—You're viewing this problem emotionally rather than rationally. While you and your business are closely related, they aren't identical. It's possible, and quite often sound practice, to market the business rather than marketing yourself. Even a personal service business can be promoted without turning the principal into a media personality. That being said, if you're in a business that deals with the public and you're uncomfortable with strangers you're going to have lots of problems. No matter how big your family or how large your circle of friends, at some point you're going to need to reach beyond your immediate circle to get customers and clients.

Become an expert—Become a student of marketing. See "Won't it cost a fortune?"

Create an environment of trust—Trust isn't an issue here. You can solve your problem by defining your situation rationally and then becoming an expert.

Turn no into yes—There isn't a need for an appeal since the no is inside your own head.

I'll look pushy (or) It's unsophisticated.

What's your problem?—Your real problem is you don't understand the nature of marketing: it needn't be a blatantly direct sales pitch.

One problem at a time—This is single problem.

Focus on facts, not feelings—You're viewing this problem emotionally rather than rationally. Marketing consists of far more than "hard sell" advertising. Much of what you can do to promote yourself will give you an even more refined image in a very subtle way. You could simply wear better suits, or buy better stationery. You could publish an article in a peer-reviewed professional journal. Sponsoring a program on your local public television or radio station, or donating to a local theater or concert group can give you a cultured image in an eminently tasteful manner.

Become an expert—Become a student of marketing. See "Won't it cost a fortune?"

Create an environment of trust—Trust isn't an issue here. You can solve your problem by defining your situation rationally and then becoming an expert.

Turn no into yes—There isn't a need for an appeal, since the no is inside your own head.

I won't have the time.

What's your problem?—Your real problem is you don't understand the nature of marketing: it's not something you do when you have the time, it's an essential element of your business and should be a fixed part of your schedule.

One problem at a time—This is single problem.

Focus on facts, not feelings—You're viewing this problem emotionally rather than rationally. If you spend all your time "doing" work, and none "getting" work, you'll soon run out of work to do. You need to realize that if you want to succeed, "getting" work must be as much a part of your work as anything else. If you don't spend a regular portion of your schedule on marketing you'll eventually be forced to throw yourself into a full-time marketing program. If you don't integrate marketing into your daily or weekly business life, then you'll find your business, and income, running in fits and starts.

Become an expert—Become a student of marketing. See "Won't it cost a fortune?"

Create an environment of trust—Trust isn't an issue here. You can solve your problem by defining your situation rationally and then becoming an expert.

Turn no into yes—There isn't a need for an appeal, since the no is inside your own head.

What if I get more work than I can handle?

What's your problem?—Your real problem is you don't understand the nature, not just of marketing, but also of leveraging your skills or finances. You're putting a roadblock in your own path to success. Having more work than you can handle, or selling more products than you yourself can produce, simply means you need to either farm out work or production.

One problem at a time—This is single problem.

Focus on facts, not feelings—You're viewing this problem emotionally rather than rationally. Having launched a small business, perhaps just a one-person operation, you're afraid of getting any larger. The fact is that your business's share of a market can either grow or it can shrink, it cannot just stay the same. That would be like playing a game not to lose. Either you can continually reach out for a larger share of your existing market, and expand your operation to match it, or you can charge more and try to get a larger share of a smaller, but more profitable, market. The moment you stop trying to get more business, you'll run yourself out of business.

Become an expert—Become a student of marketing. See "Won't it cost a fortune?"

Create an environment of trust—Trust isn't an issue here. You can solve your problem by defining your situation rationally and then becoming an expert.

Turn no into yes—There isn't a need for an appeal, since the no is inside your own head.

Borrowing Working Capital   **26**

When a man is going to try to borrow money, it is wise to look prosperous.

Benjamin Disraeli

It's easier to borrow working capital than most entrepreneurs realize . . . as long as you're borrowing it for the right reasons. Working capital loans are short-term (less than one-year) infusions of cash designed either to smooth out seasonal irregularities in your cash flow, or to provide you with the up-front cash you need to fill an order or commission. They are not quick fixes for a failing business. Understanding that is the first key step in successfully obtaining a working capital loan. The second key is to become an expert, not just in your own business, but also in the needs of any lenders you're going to approach.

Banks want to make these loans. Done properly, they're relatively safe and extremely profitable. But the banker needs to see evidence that you're able and willing to repay whatever loan he makes. The judgment on your business's ability to pay back the loan will be based on its financial track record. Your business's willingness to pay back the loan will be gauged by its credit history and the banker's estimate of your character.

Bankers are, by and large, very conservative people. Most will judge your character by the seriousness with which you treat the loan process.

That means they expect to see you dressed as if you were appearing in court. Treat the meeting casually and the banker will believe that you're going to treat your financial obligation casually as well.

All of the typical working capital loan difficulties can be either expectant or extant problems. One further note: it's always better to face up to expectant working capital problems, and address them immediately, than it is to try to deal with them as extant problems through appeals. When you can answer a banker's objection before he even raises it, you demonstrate expertise and professionalism, both of which go a long way to creating the trust you'll need to get the loan.

My track record isn't long enough.
What's your problem?—If your business hasn't been around long enough to have broken even and then managed one downturn, this is a real problem; otherwise it's a presenting problem masking some emotional or psychological reason for not wanting to borrow the funds.

One problem at a time—This is a single problem.

Focus on facts, not feelings—This isn't a judgment of your character or your business's quality; it's simply an objective decision that banks make about when a small business becomes "bankable." It is an entirely rational problem.

Become an expert—Clearly, the important piece of information to obtain is how long of a track record a particular banker needs to see to make a loan. It's very simple to obtain that and any other objective lending criteria. Just ask the banker before you apply for a loan. Remember, bankers want to make these loans. They don't want to hand out rejections. In order to prevent that, they'll do all they can to provide you with the information you need to prequalify your business and address any potential gaps in your loan application.

Create an environment of trust—Because your business doesn't have a long track record, a banker isn't going to feel confident trusting it with a working capital loan. The way to get around this dilemma is to give the banker somewhere else to put his trust.

If you're seeking the loan to smooth out your seasonal cash flow you could offer to provide a personal guarantee for the business loan or to put up some collateral. You could also have someone else who is more "bankable" serve as guarantor of the loan.

If you're going to be using the loan to help fill a large order, you can ask the banker to put his trust in your customer. Let's say you're a small fledgling parts manufacturer who has just signed on to deliver a considerable number of units to a very large established company. You can use that large established company's track record as the basis for a loan by assigning your claims against the customer to the lender. In effect, you're using your accounts receivable as collateral.

Turn no into yes—A banker is sometimes required to tell you why your loan application was rejected. And even in circumstances in which he's not so required, he'll almost always respond honestly to a direct question. Remember: the bank wants to make loans. If you were rejected because your business didn't have a sufficient track record, you can ask for a reconsideration based on the new facts that you're willing to personally guarantee the loan, obtain a third-party guarantor, put up collateral, or assign your receivables with the customer. Begin by apologizing to the banker for your lack of adequate preparation prior to submitting the loan application. Thank him for his time and efforts, and then ask his advice on which new fact would make the best impression on his loan committee. By soliciting his opinion you're treating him as a mentor and stand a good chance of getting him to act as your advocate in the process.

My credit isn't good enough.

What's your problem?—If you don't have a spotless credit record, or if your business hasn't yet established credit, this is a real problem. If you have good personal credit and your business has a long established credit line this is a presenting problem masking some emotional or psychological reason for not wanting to borrow the funds.

One problem at a time—This is a single problem, even if you have multiple problems with your credit report.

Focus on facts, not feelings—This is a completely rational problem.

Become an expert—Before applying for any loan you should become an expert on your personal and business credit files and do all you can to make them as positive as possible. Contact the major business and personal credit bureaus and order copies of your files. Check for mistakes and negative characterizations. Request that any mistakes be corrected. The burden of proof here lies with the credit bureau. If they cannot confirm information that you've questioned, then it must be corrected. Characterizations, on the other hand, can only be changed by the creditor making them. You can ask the creditor to change its judgment if you think it's unjust. You can also submit a one-hundred-word exculpatory statement which will, by law, be included in your personal credit file.

If your business doesn't yet have a credit history, find out from the banker what will be needed to establish business credit. Generally you'll need to provide some form of security for a specified period of time, after which the business's credit is established, and the security can be removed.

Create an environment of trust—If you or your business has poor or no credit, a banker will not feel comfortable trusting you, however impeccable your personal presentation. To establish that trust and obtain your working capital loan you'll need to provide the banker with somewhere else to place his trust. If you're going to be using the loan to smooth out seasonal cash flow, then you could use collateral, your personal guarantee, or a third-party guarantee. If you're planning to use the loan to fulfill a large order, you can offer to assign your accounts receivable to compensate for your poor or nonexistent credit.

Turn no into yes—A banker is, by law, required to tell you why your loan application was rejected. If you were rejected because of your poor or nonexistent credit, you can ask for a reconsideration based on the new facts that you're willing to personally guarantee the loan, obtain a third-party guarantor, put up collateral, or assign your claim against a customer. Begin by apologizing to the banker for your lack of adequate preparation prior to submitting the loan application. Thank him for his time and efforts, and then ask his advice on which new fact would make the best impression on his loan committee. By soliciting his opinion you're treating him as a mentor and stand a good chance of getting him to act as your advocate in the process.

I'm too small.

What's your problem?—This is always a presenting problem. As long as a business is bankable, size doesn't matter. There are lenders for every size business. Your actual problem is that you're too small for this particular bank.

One problem at a time—This is single problem.

Focus on facts, not feelings—Don't treat this as a reflection of your own worth. In fact, all it's indicative of is the bank's business philosophy.

Become an expert—Bankers will be just as up-front about their institution's lending strategy as they will be about loan criteria. Describe your business and your needs to the banker and ask if you are his bank's type of customer. If you're not, ask him to recommend another bank for you.

Create an environment of trust—Trust won't be an issue if you're simply not the type of customer a bank is interested in.

Turn no into yes—I don't believe it's worthwhile to try to turn this no around. You could try to convince the banker that you'll soon grow into a bigger business, but why bother? There are lots of regional and local banks that are looking to establish relationships with small businesses. The Podunk Bank of Savings hands out the same dollar bills as Citibank. In the long run you'll do better banking with an institution that wants your business.

Renegotiating Loans   **27**

Never give up. The bankers and financial people did not take me seriously initially. Everyone thought I would fail. My attitude was that "No" is an unacceptable answer when it comes to financing.

Debbi Fields

One of the biggest intellectual jumps most of my small-business clients need to make is understanding that loans aren't etched in stone. When they realize the terms of loans can, and often should, be renegotiated, and that the hurdles associated with renegotiation are surmountable, a whole new world of business opportunity is revealed.

I tell my clients to renegotiate business loans in four circumstances:

1. **they didn't borrow as much as needed to achieve their goals;**
2. **interest rates have fallen and they're stuck with a high interest loan;**
3. **they've discovered they can't continue to pay the loan back as scheduled; or**
4. **they're about to violate some condition of the loan.**

The first three scenarios are straightforward, but the fourth requires some explanation. Bankers like to make loans and then forget about them. To do that, they need to take extra precautions when making business loans of longer than one year. To protect themselves, especially when making unsecured loans, they require assurances that your business will remain in as good a fiscal condition or better than it was at the time they made the loan. To obtain those guarantees they write affirmative and negative covenants into loan agreements.

An affirmative covenant is a promise that you will do something, while a negative covenant is a promise that you won't do something. For instance, an affirmative covenant would be that you agree to maintain an assets-to-liability ratio of two to one, and a negative covenant would be that you promise not to borrow from anyone else without the lender's prior consent.

According to the terms of most loan agreements, when one of these covenants is broken, the entire loan can automatically come due, depending on the significance of the event. If, whether by design or default, your business may be violating one of the covenants of your loan agreement, you need to renegotiate the loan before the event, in order to forestall having to pay off the entire loan balance immediately.

In fact, as soon as you detect any sign of potential trouble with your loan, you should get in touch with your banker. You will not be able to keep your trouble secret from your banker. He will learn about it, one way or another. You'll have a far better chance of renegotiating if you bring the matter to his attention and present him with a plan, than if you wait for it to become obvious.

Ironically, you have the most leverage with a banker when you are in, or soon will be in, some kind of financial trouble. A banker doesn't want to write off a loan and will do almost anything to keep from doing so. Note that I said *almost anything*, not *anything*. A banker will be surprisingly flexible as long as he sees you have a chance to survive. However, he'll cut you off the moment he believes your business has no chance to make it.

You have the least leverage with a banker when you want to renegotiate simply in order to improve your bottom line; let's say you want to take advantage of dropped interest rates. The way to increase your leverage in those situations is to suggest you may consider taking your banking business elsewhere. To get a banker to renegotiate your loan down to a lower rate you'll need to have another bank's offer of a loan at that rate in your pocket.

They've turned down my request to renegotiate my loan.

What's your problem?—This is an actual problem.

One problem at a time—This is a single problem.

Focus on facts, not feelings—Remember, they've made a business decision based on the facts submitted. This isn't a personal rejection of you. In order to turn this into a rational problem you need to be more specific and determine why they have turned you down.

Become an expert—Obviously, it's vital you know your own business inside out. It's almost as important to become an expert on the banker's needs and wants. But the single most important piece of information is the reason for your rejection. Thankfully, every institutional lender, by law, must provide you with the reason for a rejection.

Create an environment of trust—It's important to always maintain a trusting relationship with your banker. It's doubly important if you're coming to him to admit that you're in trouble and need his help to survive. The banker will be looking closely at you as well as your numbers to insure you really do have a chance to pull out of your death spiral. That means you must project enthusiasm and excitement about the future, despite the current difficulty. You must also have a plan that makes sense. Even though you've been rejected you need to keep a positive outlook. The future of your business is bright. All you need is to get through the current rain squall until you reach the rainbow. You need the banker to see that light at the end of the tunnel as clearly as you do.

Turn no into yes—A banker generally will reject a request to renegotiate for one of three reasons: he doesn't have the authority to renegotiate; he no longer has confidence in your numbers; or he no longer has confidence in your ability to run the business.

If the banker says he doesn't have the authority to renegotiate, what he's really saying is he doesn't want to bring the matter to his boss and be forced to admit he made a mistake. Instead, he's trying to intimidate you into sticking to your original agreement. In this case, apologize to the banker. Say that you know you've put him in a tight spot and that you've let him down. Explain that you'll understand if he doesn't want to be your advocate, but that you at least need him to introduce you to his superior so you can present your own case. You're giving the banker a choice to either have control of the presentation to his superior or to leave it to you. Odds are he'll choose to become your advocate, if for no other reason than to protect himself.

When a banker no longer has confidence in your numbers, you need to provide him with somewhere else to place his confidence. Ask for a reconsideration based on a new proposal, this one including additional collateral and either your own personal guarantee or a third-party guarantee. As soon as the discussion shifts to the size of the collateral and the nature of the guarantees you will have succeeded in turning the no around.

A banker who no longer has confidence in you must be presented with someone else on whom he can rely. In order to turn this no around you'll need to bring in another person. It could be a new financial officer you've just hired, a general manager, a new experienced partner, or maybe even a business consultant. Whoever it is, she will need to generate sufficient trust in the banker to compensate for your failings. The more trust she generates, the easier it will be to turn the no around.

Expansion

28

If you want to be a big company tomorrow, start acting like one today.

Peter F. Drucker

Expanding a business is like investing in the stock market. You're taking dollars, which could be more secure elsewhere, and risking them in an effort to generate greater long-term profits. In the short term, the effort may cost you money. But the plan is that eventually it will pay off in a greater yield. Just as it's foolish to invest in the stock market in an effort to get out of debt, it's also crazy to expand a business in order to cure it of an ailment.

Even then, I encourage my clients to think twice about expanding. For an expansion to be successful it can't be ad hoc; there needs to be a plan. For instance, perhaps your business has succeeded selling trendy shoes in a college town. Is your next step to open another trendy shoe store in another college town? Or do you open a more mainstream shoe store in the same town as you're currently located? Then again, maybe you should expand your inventory to include more than just shoes. Any of these strategies could work, but thought has to be given to which plan makes the most sense.

Every fear and dilemma about expansion that my clients bring to me is a misconception masking their lack of understanding about the nature of expansion. Therefore, the solution to every problem and fear about expansion is to become an expert. You first need to know your current business and market like the back of your hand. It's essential you figure out exactly what has been the key to your success and then determine whether or not that key can be duplicated. You next must become an expert in industrial, geographic, and demographic trends. For instance, if you're planning on opening shoe stores in the Sunbelt, maybe you'd be better off specializing in comfortable walking shoes for aging baby boomers rather than platform sandals and Dr. Martens. Finally, you need to become an expert in management. It takes a different personality and a new set of skills to run two retail stores than it does to manage one.

I'm afraid I won't have a life if I expand the business.

What's your problem?—This is a presenting problem. Your real problem is that you're afraid you won't be able to let go of the reins and delegate authority if you expand the business.

One problem at a time—This is a single problem.

Focus on facts, not feelings—It's not uncommon for entrepreneurs to have trouble making the switch to become managers; and make no mistake about it, once you expand you must become a real manager. Your feeling undoubtedly is that you can make the switch, but in order to make a rational decision you need to look at the issue in another way: do you *want* to adopt a different role?

Become an expert—In addition to becoming an expert in your business, industry, and market, and the relevant geographic and demographic trends, you also need to become an expert in the alternatives to expansion. Rather than expanding this business you could sell it and start another. Alternatively, you could extract all the profits from this business and use them to fund another business, which you then spend most of your time launching. When the new business is ready to stand on its own you can simply fold the old one. Either is just as valid a business strategy as expansion, and both are more in tune with an entrepreneurial personality.

Create an environment of trust—Since the no is in your own head there's no need to generate trust.

Turn no into yes—There's no outright rejection here for you to appeal.

Won't I lose profits if I expand?

What's your problem?—This is a presenting problem. The real problem generally is that you don't feel comfortable investing your ready cash in a long-term project.

One problem at a time—This is a single problem.

Focus on facts, not feelings—Rather than focusing on the hypothetical loss of capital you need to instead look at the specific numbers and make a rational decision based on them, rather than on abstract fears.

Become an expert—In addition to becoming an expert in your business, industry, and market, and the relevant geographic and demographic trends, you also need to become an expert in the finances of expansion. Speak with your industry contacts and use their input to develop a detailed plan. Then, sit down with your accountant and develop an accurate breakdown of exactly how much the expansion will cost and how long it will take. Turn next to the finances of your current operation, and determine what the effect will be of drawing down the funds you need for the expansion. Be conservative in all these estimates, creating a built-in margin for error. Study the numbers carefully. Get input from your family, friends, staff, professionals, mentors, suppliers, vendors, and even friendly competitors. Focus on the additional investment of time that will be required.

Create an environment of trust—Since the no is in your own head there's no need to generate trust.

Turn no into yes—There's no outright rejection here for you to appeal.

Won't service fall off if I expand?

What's your problem?—This is a presenting problem. Generally the actual problem is that you're afraid you won't be able to find staff people who provide customer service up to your standards.

One problem at a time—This is single problem.

Focus on facts, not feelings—You are never going to find a clone of yourself. As the owner of the business you have more of a stake than anyone else could have. Instead, simply try to find good staff people who you can teach to provide excellent service.

Become an expert—In addition to becoming an expert in your business, industry, and market, and the relevant geographic and demographic trends, you also need to become a management expert, skilled in the hiring and training of staff. Seek out and speak with the owners of businesses whose staffs you find impressive. Ask them how they hire and train. If you don't feel you have the skills or patience to be a good human resources executive, consider farming out the task. Head-hunters can be used to poach your competitors' best people. Contact human resources and sales force training consultants and investigate their services. If you decide you'll need to hire professional help just make sure you factor the added cost into your projections.

Create an environment of trust—Since the no is in your own head there's no need to generate trust.

Turn no into yes—There's no outright rejection here for you to appeal.

Outsourcing

29

You will certainly not be able to take the lead in all things your-self. To one man a God has given deeds of war, and to another the dance, to another the lyre and song, and in another wide-sounding Zeus puts a good mind.

Homer

Outsourcing has probably done more to professionalize small busi-nesses than any other recent trend or invention, including information technology. The concept is a simple one: your business should focus on its core function and hire specialized firms to do everything else. For instance, a public relations agency should stick to doing public rela-tions and farm out its personnel, finance, and support work to other firms. The theory is that those other firms would also be concentrating on their own core function, enabling them to do the work more effi-ciently and better than you ever could. The net result should be that by outsourcing you will get better results for less money: an unbeat-able combination.

In most cases, the theory works when put into practice. I have one client whose small advertising agency saved more than $40,000 a year by outsourcing every function that wasn't directly related to advertising. My own office has saved more than $10,000 a year by outsourcing accounts payable. And along with those savings the job is being done better.

Obviously to eliminate potential problems you need to do your research and shop around to make sure you're getting the best firm for your dollar. But you also need to keep an eye on the outsourcing firm and yourself.

Just as an employee can get complacent, so too can an outsourcing firm. You need to keep them focused on doing their best for you. While it will require less hands-on management than if you were doing the job in house, you'll still need to do some periodic oversight. And don't just focus on the work they're doing. Make it a practice to regularly solicit new bids for the outsourced work. While you don't want to switch providers every six months, you also don't want to pay more than the market price.

Watch out for your own complacency too. It's very easy to stop paying attention to areas of your business that you've outsourced. For instance, when all my bills were paid in house I scrutinized every invoice before it was paid. I was able to instantly spot even small problems. Once I had outsourced the function I stopped being as vigilant. The firm I've hired is very good, but they're used to looking for larger problems, they look after the dollars rather than the cents. As a result I found my bills slowly creeping upward. Since spotting this trend myself I've started being more vigilant. I don't check every bill as I used to, but once a quarter I take the monthly bills home and spend a weekend studying them.

It will cost too much.

What's your problem?—If you've done the research and have found that it will cost you more to outsource than to do the work in house then you've uncovered a real problem. If, on the other hand, you're just assuming it would cost more, this is a presenting problem. You're actually just afraid of delegating the authority.

One problem at a time—This is a single problem.

Focus on facts, not feelings—If you've done your research this is a rational problem. After all, one reason for outsourcing is to save money. If, however, you're just making an assumption, this is an emotional problem. Get some specifics. How much will it cost? How much more is that than what you're paying now?

Become an expert—Double-check your numbers. Make sure you've accurately estimated your current costs. If necessary, have your accountant do the calculations. Next, look for more outsourcing firms. Perhaps you've only gotten bids from the most expensive players in the market. Leave no stone unturned. At this point your goal is simply to find out what the market rate is for the service.

If it appears that no outsourcing firm will offer direct cost savings, determine whether the firm's more efficient operations will offer indirect savings, not just in dollars but in freeing up personnel schedules.

Create an environment of trust—It's the outsourcing firm's job to get you to trust them.

Turn no into yes—If you've thoroughly investigated the issue and have found that no outsourcing firm can do the work for the same as or less than you're currently paying, or create any cost savings or labor savings through efficiency, keep the function in house. Don't outsource a function simply because it's the trendy thing to do.

If you find that the firm you'd like to take on the task is charging more than you're paying now, and that their fee is above the market value, ask them to reconsider their bid. Offer up your research and note that you'd love for them to do the work, but you can't justify their retention in light of the facts you've uncovered.

They'll estrange my customers.

What's your problem?—This is a presenting problem. Your actual problem is that you haven't accurately defined the core elements of your business.

One problem at a time—This is a single problem.

Focus on facts, not feelings—This is an entirely rational problem, unless of course you're hiring the outsourcing firm to handle customer relations. That would be shocking.

Become an expert—The solution here is to only consider outsourcing those functions that don't require interaction with customers. You need to reexamine your definition of what your core function is. I'd urge you to consider any area of your business in which you deal with customers or clients as the core of your business. Without customers and clients you have nothing. They are your most precious resource.

Create an environment of trust—While it's the outsourcing firm's job to get you to trust them, getting your clients or customers to trust you remains one of your most important tasks.

Turn no into yes—There's no need to turn this no around. If you've made a mistake in defining your core business, simply start over with a new definition.

I'll lose quality control.

What's your problem?—This is an actual problem.

One problem at a time—This is a single problem.

Focus on facts, not feelings—This is also entirely rational—believe me, I know firsthand.

Become an expert—Make sure you've done a top-notch job of researching, interviewing, and checking up on all the candidate firms. Carefully go over exactly what services each will provide and the procedures they'll follow. Look for steps in the process when you will have a chance to check up on their work. Query their other clients or customers.

Create an environment of trust—Ironically, this is a problem where you don't want to have too much trust in another party. Explain that while you trust the firm to do a good job, you need to have some oversight role in the process. Say that you're not looking to control them, only to keep a watchful eye on the bottom line. You may want to hint that the level of your oversight could diminish over time as you become more comfortable with them. Also, insist on their conducting internal oversight as well. Remember, the person who brings you into their company may concentrate only on marketing.

Turn no into yes—There's no appeal involved in this problem.

Soliciting Equity Investors

30

> Nowhere is a man's imagination so fertile as in the discovery of
> new ways to say no to a man who asks for money.
>
> *Joseph H. Shapiro*

The most difficult task facing any small business owner is trying to
solicit equity investors. You're asking people to make long-term, illiq-
uid, risky investments in your business while offering little if any say
in how the business is run. In effect, you're asking them to become
silent partners. Is it any wonder so few people say yes?

There are two secrets to successfully recruiting equity investors.
First, you must become an expert on the people you are approaching.
You need to know their risk aversion and needs in order to tailor your
proposal to fit them. Most of all, you need to know that they actually
have the funds to invest. That's because the second secret to successfully recruiting investors is to realize you'll almost always be rejected
initially, and the one reason for a no that cannot be turned into a yes is
"I don't have the money."

They turned me down.
What's your problem?—This is your real, and probably all too
common, problem.
One problem at a time—This is single problem.

Focus on facts, not feelings—This is also a rational problem, as long as you view it as a rejection of your loan proposal, rather than of you as a human being.

Become an expert—In order to convince someone to invest in your business you must be seen as the ultimate expert in its past, present, and future. You need to know your business plan inside and out. You must have an answer to every possible question, no matter how insightful or inane. But that's not enough. You also need to know all there is to know about the person you're approaching. Does he have sufficient funds to invest? Has he invested in businesses like yours before? How did those investments turn out? What kind of investments turn him on or off? Is he looking for a good return on his investment in a short period of time? Or is he interested in long-term growth? Has he shown a proclivity for taking risks, or is he risk adverse? Who are his accountant and investment advisor? Does he have experience in managing a business? Does he have experience in a business like yours? Can he help influence other investors to come aboard? Is he a "giver" or a "taker"?

Create an environment of trust—Your incredibly detailed knowledge of your business can serve as a foundation for trust, but it won't be sufficient to land an investment. You not only need to treat the potential investor with respect and care, but you must also convey that you'll take better care of his money than you would your own. All of your personal trust building won't be enough, however. You'll also need to bring in outside factors to document what you've said. Market surveys can help. Certified financial statements are a definite plus. Outside reports from marketing consultants and industry analysts will add meat to your claims. Most impressive are any third-party endorsements of your business plan. You need to do everything you can to create enough trust in just one single investor. Once you break the ice you won't need to be as desperate.

It's always easier to get the second investor than it is the first. There's a bandwagon effect that takes place among small-business investors. When one investor has demonstrated faith in your plan by signing on, it encourages others to do the same. Rather than taking a risk on an unknown, they'll see it as getting in on the ground floor of a great deal.

Turn no into yes—To find out why a potential investor has said no you'll need to ask him. Unfortunately, not everyone will tell you the truth. In fact, most will fudge their answer for one reason or another. They may not want to hurt your feelings. Or they may not want to reveal their lack of knowledge. Whatever the case, you may need to read between the lines and chase down outside leads to get a true reading on the reason.

If you sense or learn that the potential investor didn't understand your plan, you need to subtly get around their deficiency without damaging their pride. I've found that the best way to do that is to ask to meet with their accountant or investment advisor as soon as you see that a no is coming. Explain that there are some additional intricacies about the deal that you need to discuss, but that you don't want to bore him with the details. Then, ask for permission to contact his advisors. You're almost sure to get the okay, since the investor sees it as a way to spare himself from having to say no. Once you're in touch with the investment advisor you'll have a chance to pitch a more informed audience, or discover some undisclosed obstacle.

If you sense or learn that the potential investor thought your plan was too risky, you'll need to alter your proposal. Perhaps you can offer them a surer exit from the deal. You can offer to buy them out over a period of time at an acceptable yield (that's called a "put"), or to have someone else buy them out. You could also offer them a hybrid deal. Tell them that if they make a five-year loan to the company, when it comes due—or sooner at their option—you'll give them the choice of turning the loan into equity, or getting back their funds with interest. Remember, getting that first investor is the key. Be as flexible as you can be now, and you won't need to be as flexible in the future.

If you sense or learn that the potential investor didn't feel he would have enough input into decision making, come back with a further explanation of how you'll be reporting. Explain that you'll be acting as responsibly as if you were a public company. Say that you'll be giving him updates on operations every ninety days, at which time you'll be asking for his feedback, and your accountant will give him a comprehensive financial report every six months. Interestingly enough, regular reporting is usually sufficient to preempt any investor intrusions into operations. Simply demonstrate that you respect their knowledge and the vital role they play in your business and they'll be happy.

If you sense or learn that the potential investor didn't believe in either your numbers or your ability to run the business, you'll need to stall for time. You've already put them through the full court press. Nothing you do or say at this point will make them change their mind. Instead, ask if you can come back to them in the future with some further information. Having turned you down once already they'll happily agree to giving you another audience just to ease their own guilt. Rather than trying to alter your plan or presentation, come back to this potential investor when you have another already signed up. The only thing that will turn around a no based on lack of faith in you or your numbers is that another investor has faith in you and your numbers.

Selling a Business

31

There are two kinds of statistics, the kind you look up and the kind you make up.

Rex Stout, Death of a Doxy

Few entrepreneurs run their business with the intent of selling it. Most people, especially the owners of small businesses, run their operations with an eye toward bettering their current personal financial situation, maximizing their cash intake, and minimizing their tax bill. That's fine for a time. After all, while income tax evasion is illegal, income tax avoidance is downright patriotic. But if you do decide to sell your business, and you've run it in this manner, you'll be facing a problem. Simply put, tax minimization can affect your business's apparent viability.

All of your business's documentation and records show the maximum expenses and perhaps deferred income. Now that it's time to sell, you want to do the opposite: play down your expenses and play up your income. That means buyers will be faced with a choice: they can believe you or they can believe your numbers. Unless you're desperate to sell quickly, don't care about getting what your business is actually worth, or are prepared to take cash for its book value, you're going to have to do something dramatic to get the buyer to go along with your stated rather than reported numbers. You can try to help the buyer and her professional team analyze your records in a way that lends credence to your statements, but that's rarely enough. Any savvy buyer will adopt the cold war adage: "trust but verify." The solution is for you to take back paper.

The compromise is generally that the seller takes back a note equal to the amount of value that cannot be documented. The note comes due at an agreed upon point when the buyer can see from the operations of the business that the seller's claims about income were, in fact, accurate. If the claims don't hold water, the note is canceled and the sale is made entirely on the basis of the documented numbers. It sounds complex, but it's a process hundreds of people go through each and every day with the assistance of accountants and lawyers who specialize in just this type of transaction. Their fees are the price you'll have to pay for having run your business more like a mom-and-pop shop rather than a multinational corporation.

They don't believe my claims.

What's your problem?—This is an actual problem.

One problem at a time—This is a single problem.

Focus on facts, not feelings—This is an entirely rational problem. Hey, if you were buying a business you wouldn't believe the seller's claims either.

Become an expert—Sit down with your accountant or a business valuation expert and determine the actual value of your business. Compare that to its book value. Analyze your business and personal records and numbers to see if there are any ways you can help justify, if not prove, the claims you're making. Finally, meet with your attorney to explore ways you can structure the sale so as to get your business's true worth.

Create an environment of trust—Even though no buyer is going to trust you enough to pay cash for your business's claimed but undocumented value,* you still need to work hard to create an environment of trust. While she may not be paying the full price in cash, she really is buying the business on the assumption that your claim is true. It's essential you do all you can to prove your candor.

---

*Even if a buyer was naive enough to pay your price in cash, no lawyer would let her do it.

You'll need to develop a good relationship with the buyer because you may want or need to work with her for a certain period of time after the sale. Perhaps you'll want to insure she's running the business intelligently enough to make the kind of money you did and, therefore, support your claims. You might need to remain on staff and work with her because she may want your help in learning the ropes and easing the transition.

Turn no into yes—You should automatically assume you'll get this no and will need to respond with a reconsideration based on the fact that you're ready to accept paper for the amount in dispute. If the buyer refuses to pay more than book value, walk away from the deal. She's looking to steal rather than buy a business.

The landlord will object (or) The landlord has objected.

What's your problem?—If your lease gives the landlord the right to approve assignments or sublets, this is an actual problem . . . whether it's expectant or extant.

One problem at a time—This is a single problem.

Focus on facts, not feelings—This is also entirely rational. The landlord looks at transitions in tenants as opportunities to increase rent. If you assign your lease he's missing out on that increase. In addition, he may have developed confidence in your business's ability to pay the rent. The new owner is an unknown quantity.

Become an expert—If you are planning on selling and you didn't successfully negotiate a flexible enough assignability clause when you first signed the lease, you need to go back and renegotiate one now. Bring in your attorney as your hired gun and do whatever you can to change the lease so it smoothes the way for you to sell.

Create an environment of trust—Theoretically the landlord already trusts you. Your mission now should be to get him to trust your buyer as well. Do everything you can to demonstrate to the landlord that he'll actually be in a better position with this new tenant than with you. For instance, if she's younger than you, that would guarantee him more years of continued occupancy; or if she has "deep pockets" that could make it easier for him to increase the rent when the lease expires.

Turn no into yes—The only further fact you can add if you need to ask for a reconsideration is that you will serve as personal guarantor of the lease for part of the remaining term, or the new owner can offer an increase in the security deposit.

My employees will bolt.
What's your problem?—This is an actual problem.
One problem at a time—This is a single problem.
Focus on facts, not feelings—This is also entirely rational. Seasoned employees know that wholesale staff changes almost always come close on the heels of changes in ownership and management. The minute that word leaks that you're thinking of selling, your best people will become flight risks.

Become an expert—The key information you need to gather is actually from the buyer, not your employees. If the buyer plans on making wholesale immediate staff changes she may not want you to stop your employees from bolting. On the other hand, if she wants to hold on to people, at least for a little while, she'll be helpful in solving the problem.

Create an environment of trust—Your employees, understandably, aren't going to trust any verbal promises from either you or the future owner. Even though they trust you, they also know that you won't be around much longer, and that your primary concern is closing the deal, not saving their skins. The solution is to sign your key employees to contracts. The difficulty is that this will be a three-way negotiation among you, the future owner, and the employee. That's why I suggest clients in this situation focus on crafting simpler termination agreements instead. These should provide sufficient security to the employees without binding the future owner's hands.

Turn no into yes—If an employee refuses to sign an agreement, you can make a personal plea for him to reconsider. Meet him privately, as a friend rather than an employer, and explain that the termination agreement won't prevent him from looking for another job. All it will do is memorialize his severance package. And since he suspects he'll be terminated shortly anyway, this is a chance for him to get more than he would have otherwise.

Part 4

Turning No into Yes When Facing Real Estate Problems

Buying

32

It takes a heap o' livin' in a house t' make it home,
A heap o' sun an' shadder, an' ye sometimes have t' roam,
Afore ye really 'preciate the things ye lef' behind,
An' hunger fer 'em somehow, wit 'em allus on yer mind.

Edgar Albert Guest, Home

Most of the home-buying problems clients bring to me have their roots in a common misconception about the real estate market. Ever since the 1980s, most people have viewed real estate as a wonderful investment. While that was true for a while, it's no longer the case.

Historically, buying real estate has been as much an emotional as a financial decision. When you owned your own home you were literally king of your own castle. No absentee landlord could raise your rent, turn off the heat, or make you put up with a leaky roof. You could grow your own food and raise your own livestock, or you could put up a trampoline and basketball hoop for your kids. You could put up knotty pine paneling in your dining room and build a workshop in the basement. You were in control. Financially, you could deduct the interest on your mortgage, and rest assured that your home's value would probably outpace inflation. If nothing else, paying a mortgage rather than rent was a form of enforced savings.

Things changed in the 1980s when the leading edge of the baby boom generation began entering the home-buying market. Because of post–World War II prosperity, federally subsidized home loans, and the development of the middle-class suburb, many baby boomers grew up in homes owned by their parents, unlike previous generations. They wanted to buy homes similar to those they'd grown up in. But because there were so many baby boomers, the demand drove prices up. Houses purchased by a boomer's parents in 1965 for $15,000 were selling in 1985 to a young boomer family for $150,000. The same demographic anomaly that forced home prices up kept salaries down in real terms. To afford to buy their parents' home, boomer couples had to bring in two salaries and spend a higher share of their income on shelter.

Prices kept soaring throughout the 1980s as more and more baby boomers entered the market. Older boomers were able to buy and sell homes quickly, make a tidy profit off younger boomers, and use the money to buy an even larger home. But then at the end of the decade the tide turned. The number of buyers began to drop, demand slowed, and prices stagnated and then fell. The age of real estate as an investment was over. But not everyone has gotten the message.

Most of the clients who come to me with real estate problems are still thinking as if it were the 1980s. It's not.* Today people should be buying a home they're willing to stay in for a long portion of their lives. They should look at it as a spiritual and emotional purchase, as more of a quality-of-life issue than a financial issue.

But it's a thirty-year debt!

What's your problem?—If this is an instinctive, and uninformed response to the prospect of taking out a mortgage, then it's your actual problem. Ironically, if it's a considered fear based on knowledge, then it's a presenting problem.

One problem at a time—This is a single problem.

Focus on facts, not feelings—This is usually an irrational fear. You're looking at a mortgage in the wrong way. While it is in some

---

*There are, however, spikes in certain areas of the country, based on the performance of Wall Street. These aren't booms, just short-term jumps when the market or a certain stock soars, followed by quick dips when the market or the same stock falls.

ways a thirty-year debt, that's an overly simplistic and emotional way to view buying a home.

First, a mortgage need not last thirty years. You can obtain fifteen-year mortgages, and most mortgages today have no prepayment penalty, meaning you can pay it off as soon as you'd like. Conversely, you can stretch the debt out for more than thirty years by refinancing whenever it makes sense.

Second, the impact of making mortgage payments should more rationally be viewed as a monthly expense rather than as a thirty-year debt. And that monthly expense isn't as daunting as it might at first seem. The interest and tax portions of your monthly payment are tax deductible. That means its impact is reduced. Also, since you're making payments on an asset you'll eventually own outright, mortgage payments aren't just expenses; they contain an element of long-term savings.

If after learning about mortgages, and viewing them as monthly expenses, you find that you're still frightened by the prospect, then you need to revisit the whole issue of buying a home. While your fear is still irrational, it's masking deeper fears, perhaps about commitment.

Become an expert—The more you can learn about mortgages the less fear you'll have. Besides speaking with bankers, pick up and read a few of the latest home-buying books in the bookstore or library. Check out the mortgage resources available on the Internet. Perhaps the best online sites are those that offer calculators that help you figure out your affordability, the tax impact of mortgage payments, and the advantages of various interest rates and terms.

Create an environment of trust—Trust isn't an issue in developing a more rational attitude toward mortgages.

Turn no into yes—There's no appeal in this problem.

Am I paying too much?

What's your problem?—This is an actual problem.

One problem at a time—This is a single problem.

Focus on facts, not feelings—Once again, this is a case of looking at the issue emotionally rather than rationally. What do you mean by too much? If you're looking to pay less than the market value for a home, then you're allowing issues of pride and ego to cloud the situation. There shouldn't be a winner and loser in this process. Your goal should be to pay as little as you can, within the market value range for the property. Remember, this isn't a short-term financial investment. It's a long-term lifestyle purchase.

Become an expert—It's actually quite easy to determine the market value range of a property. First, ask real estate brokers for "comparables." These are recent sales records of comparable, nearby homes. If a comparable but slightly more attractive property sold last week for $120,000, and a comparable, but slightly less attractive property sold the week before for $110,000, the market value for your property is $110 to $120,000. If you'd like further information, or can't easily obtain comparables yourself, consider hiring an outside expert: a real estate appraiser. An appraiser will be able to take a more scientific approach to value, getting into even greater detail. Finally, realize that if you're taking out a mortgage loan to buy a property, the lender will conduct its own appraisal before making the loan. If the lender thinks you're paying more than the market value it will say so and will refuse to make the loan, or will reduce the amount they're willing to commit. That's a built-in safety net for you.

Create an environment of trust—The more that you can rely on comparables rather than opinions and guesswork, the less you'll need to rely on your trust in the broker in determining whether or not you're overpaying. This is one case where I'd rather see you put your faith in figures.

Turn no into yes—It doesn't always make sense to appeal an appraisal that has come in for less than you thought. If the appraisal didn't involve an actual physical inspection of the property and instead was done solely by checking comparables and taking a quick peek at the house (known in the business as a "drive-by appraisal"), you can express your concerns and ask the appraiser to take a closer look. Be aware, however, that appraisers are human beings. If they sense you or the bank want a higher figure, that could influence their judgment. To compensate for that tendency, stress that your sole reason for sending them back is to get a more accurate read on value, one in which you'll have more confidence, not to get a higher or lower number.

Are you sure it's not a lemon?
What's your problem?—This is generally an actual problem.

One problem at a time—This is a single problem.

Focus on facts, not feelings—To turn this into a rational problem it is essential that you define what you mean by a lemon. Are you afraid there's something mechanically or structurally wrong that will force you into huge repair bills, or are you worried there's something esthetically wrong with the property that will make it difficult to sell in the future?

Become an expert—Fears about mechanical and structural problems can be calmed by having the property checked by a structural engineer or home inspector. Look for a licensed, full-time home inspector with the training to also conduct insect and radon, as well as structural inspections. Tag along on the inspection, asking about anything you don't understand or that concerns you. While the written report will give you all the facts, there will be much less subtext and jargon in a one-on-one conversation.

Worries about the future salability of the property can only be assuaged by becoming an expert in the past sales history of the house. The broker may be able to give you some information, but be aware that he or she is a biased source. It's in the broker's interest to make a sale. Better sources are your potential neighbors. Take a tour of the area. How does it fit in with the other properties in the area? Is it far grander than every other home on the block? Does its design make it stick out like a mortician at a clowns' convention? Knock on doors and introduce yourself. Ask about the history of the house. Has it repeatedly been on the market for long periods of time?

Create an environment of trust—If you don't have sufficient trust in your inspector to accept his report as accurate, find another inspector. If you don't have sufficient confidence in your own ability to judge a home and an area, bring along someone you trust—perhaps an objective family member or friend, or maybe even a savvy accountant or attorney.

Turn no into yes—If you find that there are indeed some mechanical problems with the home, that doesn't mean you should reject it outright. Get an estimate for how much the problems will cost to cure, and then appeal the selling price, offering your discovery and repair estimate as new facts to be considered. The idea is to lower the price of the home by the cost of the repairs.

If you discover the home does have a problematic sales history due to its uniqueness, you need to make a further self-analysis. Just because a home won't be easy to resell doesn't mean it shouldn't be purchased. Magnificent and unique structures—say, Frank Lloyd Wright's Fallingwater—will never sell quickly. However, if their uniqueness brings sufficient added joy into your life, that could more than compensate for it taking a long time to resell. It really is a personal judgment.

I've been turned down for a mortgage.

What's your problem?—This is always the real problem.

One problem at a time—This is a single problem.

Focus on facts, not feelings—Mortgage rejections are never about you, they are either about the numbers on your application or the property itself. Don't take this personally.

Become an expert—Obviously you hadn't become enough of an expert on the needs and wants of the lender, or on your own finances, before you filed your application.

Create an environment of trust—Unless you showed up looking and acting like a lunatic, your rejection probably had nothing to do with your ability to get the lender to trust you. Because they are so common and profitable, and are so often bundled together with other loans and sold to other lenders on the secondary mortgage market, bankers actually make home mortgage loans based on the application's numbers and the qualities of the property, not on the character of the borrower.

Turn no into yes—As always, the secret to winning an appeal is to find out the reason for the rejection. Bankers will nearly always tell you why your application was turned down, so you shouldn't have any problem getting this information.

If the problem is that the property was not appraised for a sufficient value, you have two avenues for appeal: the appraisal itself and the amount you're seeking as a loan. Find out if it was a "drive-by" appraisal. If it was, ask for a more in-depth investigation. If the appraisal was fairly substantive, hire your own appraiser to double-check the original findings. In the case of a variation in the appraisals, submit yours and ask for a reconsideration. When an independent appraisal verifies the bank's own finding, consider asking for a smaller loan. To protect itself a bank will only loan up to a certain percentage (usually eighty, sometimes ninety) of the house's appraised value. By asking for a smaller loan that falls within that percentage you will be able to turn a no into a yes.

If you've been rejected because you don't have sufficient assets or because of past credit problems, ask for a reconsideration based on your bringing in someone to cosign the loan as a guarantor. In effect, you are borrowing against the guarantor's net worth and good credit.

If you've been rejected because you don't show sufficient income to make the monthly payments you again have two choices. You can either ask for a smaller loan and put more money into your down payment, or you can demonstrate that you have more income coming in than was originally shown in your application. Perhaps you failed to include your freelance income or the annual cash gift you receive from your grandparents.

If you've been rejected because you already have too much outstanding debt—say student loans and credit card balances—you have yet another two choices. You can amend your application to show more income, or you can pay down the balances on your other loans.

Whatever the reason for your rejection you'll find the banker eager to help you in the appeal. Banks don't make money rejecting loans. And home mortgages are the safest and most profitable loans they make. Believe it or not, the bank wants to loan you the money.

The coop board has rejected me.

What's your problem?—This is an actual problem.

One problem at a time—This is a single problem.

Focus on facts, not feelings—I wish I could tell you that this has nothing to do with you as a human being . . . but I can't. Coop and other membership boards have been known to reject people because of what they do for a living, or even how they dress. You can be rejected just because a board member simply has taken an irrational dislike to you. As long as they're not rejecting you because of the color of your skin or some other illegal reason, they can basically reject you for any reason in most states.

Become an expert—The secret here is to become an expert on the history of the board before you appear before them. A good broker can provide you with advice on any idiosyncrasies of the board, as well as guidance on things with which they are rationally concerned. The building's or complex's managing agent may also be of some help. In addition, the seller might be able to provide some insight. This is clearly a case where it's essential to be forewarned.

Create an environment of trust—It may be annoying and inconvenient, but you really do need to treat the meeting with the board as a job interview. Dress and act like their dream neighbor: that means stable, quiet, and unobtrusive. The only thing about you that should stand out is the green of your money.

Turn no into yes—It can be very difficult to turn coop or board rejections around for two reasons: they don't have to give you a reason for saying no, and their reason can be completely irrational. Use the broker, managing agent, seller, and any contacts you might have to ferret out the reason if it's not given.

If the reason is a rational one, immediately petition the coop or group chairman for a reconsideration based on new facts that directly address the reason for your rejection. Include those facts in your request for a reconsideration, demonstrating to the chairman that you have a good case.

If the reason for your rejection is irrational you could try to point that out to the board chairman, but I don't think it's worth the effort. He or she undoubtedly already knows it was an irrational no. And if the board chose to make a decision based on emotions rather than facts, they're also unlikely to find such actions troubling. Boards who reject people for silly personal reasons are petty tyrants who won't back down in the face of facts. Rather than spend time fighting windmills, let your broker know it's his or her job to keep you from getting into these situations again, and start looking for another place.

Renovating

33

If we want things to stay as they are, things will have to change.

Giuseppe di Lampedusa, The Leopard

Up until the real estate boom of the 1980s, home renovation was an outlet for American creativity. But when buying real estate became a short-term financial investment rather than a lifestyle purchase the rules of renovation changed. Suddenly, the most important thing was recouping costs and not doing anything that might deter a potential buyer. It was the age of the plain vanilla kitchen and bathroom project. I think that age is over. Yet, that attitude is still out there, underlying nearly every renovation problem that's brought to me.

You'll have fewer home renovation fears and problems if you realize that the spiritual and emotional factors in improvements and additions now outweigh the financial factors. That doesn't mean you should go overboard and put a $80,000 kitchen in a $100,000 home. But you shouldn't hesitate to, for instance, sink some money in a pool. If it will be the focus of your family's summers for years to come you'll recoup the cost in pleasant memories rather than dollars. To me, that's a fair exchange. If you can afford it, and it will add to your enjoyment of your home without being totally outlandish (like building a tennis court alongside your trailer), go for it.

Can't costs get out of hand?

What's your problem?—This is an actual problem.

One problem at a time—This is a single problem.

Focus on facts, not feelings—This is also a rational problem.

Become an expert—The solution to this problem is to become an expert on your own project and on the details of your arrangement with your general contractor. Renovation costs do tend to get out of hand. That's for three reasons.

First, the plans may not be comprehensive, leading to unexpected costs along the way. You can avoid that pitfall by insisting your architect or designer provide complete plans. Ask all the contractors who bid on the job to point out any gaps they see in the plan. Whichever contractor is hired, bring all suspected gaps in the plans to the planner's attention.

Second, contractors often underestimate their costs. Sometimes it's because they're desperate to win the job and come in with a low bid. Other times it's because they run into a hidden surprise—say a rotted beam replacement—which throws off their estimates of material and labor. You can overcome this potential hurdle by insisting on binding bids from your contractors. While these will automatically come in higher than nonbinding bids, since the contractor needs to build in a safety net, you will at least know for sure what your project will cost.

Third, and most problematic, homeowners often make changes to their plans while the project is under way. Every change you make costs you more. Contractors, in an effort to both deter and profit from these "change orders," charge much more for these items than they would normally. For instance, adding an electrical outlet that's in your plans might cost $50, while adding one that's not planned for could cost you $100. To avoid these costly change orders, spend a great deal of time with your plans. It's far cheaper to make changes to paper than it is to Sheetrock. The more study you put into your plans the less likely you'll end up over budget.

Create an environment of trust—While you'll need to have a level of trust with your architect and general contractor, it's facts not feelings that count in these relationships. Don't rely on your relationship or on verbal assurances. Put your trust in well-crafted, ironclad agreements instead. Not only should these agreements specify costs, but they should also give a date for completion, including language requiring the work to be continuous. A specific payment schedule, tied to the work done, which lets you hold back a percentage until you're satisfied with the final result, is essential.

Turn no into yes—There's no appeal in this situation.

Will I get my money back when I sell?

What's your problem?—This is your actual problem.

One problem at a time—This is a single problem.

Focus on facts, not feelings—Ironically, even though you're focusing on the dollars rather than sentiment, this is often an emotional rather than a rational problem. If you're renovating strictly to increase the value of your home, then you're being rational worrying about your return. However, if you're renovating to improve the quality of your life, getting back every penny you put into an improvement isn't the prime issue. Instead, focus on getting the most pleasure for your money. Your return on investment should be measured in joy, not dollars.

Become an expert—If your goal is to renovate in order to improve the salability of your home you need to become an expert on what buyers in your area expect. Speak with two or three real estate brokers and get their opinions on the kind of improvements that attract buyers. Ask if there are any renovations that turn off buyers. Then, plan your projects with an eye toward creating a plain vanilla environment. Keep in mind that improvements that bring your home up to the level of others in your area will provide the best return on investment. For example, modernizing an old kitchen or bathroom will be more profitable than changing an already acceptable floor plan.

Create an environment of trust—Trust isn't a factor in this problem.

Turn no into yes—There's no appeal in this problem.

The building department rejected my plans.

What's your problem?—This is an actual problem.

One problem at a time—This is a single problem.

Focus on facts, not feelings—This isn't a rejection of you, so don't take it personally. In fact, it's not really a rejection of your plans either. It's a rejection of your architect or contractor who drew up the plans.

Become an expert—In this instance you need to rely on the expertise of others. Whichever of your professionals drew up the plans must now go back to the building department with modified or amended plans that meet their approval.

Create an environment of trust—After screwing up in this manner it's now up to your architect or contractor to recreate the environment of trust that once existed between you.

Turn no into yes—While an appeal might be necessary it should, once again, be the responsibility of your architect or contractor. He or she should be the one who approaches the building department and asks for a variance or exception, or who tries to get them to accept a different interpretation of the building code.

Renting

34

And my parents finally realize that I'm kidnapped and they snap
into action immediately: They rent out my room.

Woody Allen

Home or apartment rental problems can almost all be solved the same
way: having an ironclad lease. The best way to avoid expectant problems is to make sure your fear is addressed in the lease. Extant problems can also best be cured by holding the other party to the terms of
the lease.

Residential leases, while less complex than commercial agreements,
are still complicated enough to require an attorney. In fact, I tell all
my clients who are contemplating becoming landlords to hire professionals to oversee the entire process. Unless you plan on getting into
the real estate business full-time you don't have the time to do the
kind of job that's required to insure your interests are fully protected.
Leave the drafting of the lease to your lawyer and the screening of tenants to an agent. All you should have to do is deposit the rent check
on the first of the month.

Won't the tenants create damage?
What's your problem?—This is your actual problem.
One problem at a time—This is a single problem.

Focus on facts, not feelings—This is an entirely rational problem. Tenants almost always create damage, just as any residents will. You must expect a certain amount of wear and tear anytime property is used.

Become an expert—In order to mitigate damage problems you must express your concerns to your attorney when she is preparing the lease. She can insure that your lease requires an adequate security deposit, insist that no changes can be made to the property without your approval, and provide you or your agent with the right to make occasional formal inspections of the premises.

You also need to make your worries plain to your renting agent. He must be prepared to make a real judgment of the tenant's character, and to check their references and background. In addition, get the agent's input on what type of restrictions make sense. After all, a family of four with two pets will create more damage than a couple with no pets.

Create an environment of trust—In this situation it's the prospective tenant's role to create the environment of trust with both you and your agent. You, on the other hand, should insist on your trust being reinforced by an airtight lease agreement.

Turn no into yes—There's no appeal in this situation.

What if I can't get them out?

What's your problem?—This is an actual problem.

One problem at a time—This is a single problem.

Focus on facts, not feelings—As anyone who has ever tried to evict a tenant can tell you, this is an entirely rational problem. It is very difficult to get someone out of a residence, even if they haven't paid rent. In many states, the law bends over backward to protect the tenant at the landlord's expense. This is one reason why I don't encourage my clients to get into the rental business.

Become an expert—You can never totally protect yourself from this happening. A tenant who interviewed well, and who was reliable for years, can suddenly change and become a problem. All you can do is mitigate the problem. First, make sure you have an experienced agent do the screening, looking out for potential problem tenants. Second, ask your lawyer to do everything possible to keep a recalcitrant tenant from barricading himself in your property. She may be able to construct the lease so that tenants become trespassers if they overstay, allowing you to enlist the aid of the police in having them removed.

Create an environment of trust—It is the tenant who must create an environment of trust in order to get you to give him possession of your property. Landlords need to put their trust in the strength of their lease.

Turn no into yes—There is no appeal in this situation.

Selling   35

Everything is worth what its purchaser will pay for it.

Publilius Syrus

Most home-selling problems stem mostly from greed. People want to get top dollar in what is one of the biggest transactions they'll ever make. While that's understandable, it's foolish. As I pointed out in the buying and renovating chapters, real estate simply is no longer a short-term investment. Besides, the value of owning your home is made up of far more than just the profit you make on its sale. During the years when you had a mortgage on your home you were able to take advantage of the deductibility of home mortgage interest. You also were able to "save" the dollars you paid in mortgage principle, rather than "spending" it as you would have had you been a renter. Finally, and most importantly, you were able to get all the emotional, spiritual, and psychological benefits of ownership. In effect, you had a home rather than just a house.

I tell my clients that their goals should be to quickly sell their home for its market value. I suggest they place as much if not more emphasis on the speed of the sale rather than the size of the price. The sooner you sell the sooner you can move on with your life and/or earn interest on the proceeds from the sale.

What if I can't sell? (or) **I'm afraid of losing money.**

What's your problem?—This is your actual problem.

One problem at a time—This is a single problem.

Focus on facts, not feelings—These are both irrational problems. There are few homes, if any, that can't be sold . . . for the right price. Every market has periods when demand is down and supply is up, yet sales still take place. How? The seller lowers his price to the point where his product becomes more attractive than the alternatives. To make this into a rational problem you need to be more specific. Instead of asking "What if I can't sell?" it makes better sense to ask "What if I can't sell for as much as I want?" The solution to that question is easy: you lower your price.

Losing money on the sale of your home would indeed be a shame. And while it would have an economic impact, worrying about it is still irrational. That's because there's really nothing you can do about it. If the current market value for your home is less than it was when you bought the house, you will indeed get less than you paid. You may have added many improvements to the property, but if your home was already at the top end of its value range when you bought it you may not even get back the money you put into it. To make this into a rational problem you need to be more specific and focus, not on getting back what you paid for the home, but on getting as much as you possibly can. The only people who "lose money" on real estate are those who are in the real estate business and who don't get any use or emotional benefit from the property. You need to balance the time it takes to sell and the price you're getting.

Become an expert—In order to put the right price on your home you need to become an expert on your local real estate market. Ask at least three or four brokers to visit your home and give you an estimate of its value in today's market. Make sure they back up their estimates by citing the recent sales of comparable properties.

Study those comparables and see how your home measures up. Is your street nicer than the street of the similar home that sold for $125,000? Are the rooms in your home smaller than those in the similar house that sold for $140,000? Unlike the comparables, do you have a new furnace and roof? The idea is to determine not an exact price but a range of value, and then to estimate where within that range your home falls. Realize that homes at the upper end of the range will take longer to sell than homes at the lower end of the range.

Don't immediately sign with the broker who gives you the highest estimate. He may be overestimating in order to get your listing. It's not uncommon for brokers to first talk up a home's value, and then after a bid comes in, hammer on the owner to come down in price dramatically.

Stress to the brokers that you're interested in a speedy sale, and ask for their suggestions on what you can do to your home to make it more salable. New neutral paint schemes and some minor cosmetic steps—like thinning out your furniture and adding some strategically placed mirrors—coupled with an attractive price may make the difference between a home that sells in a week and one that lingers on the market for a year.

Create an environment of trust—You need to place your trust not in your broker but in the magic of the marketplace. Do everything you reasonably can to make your home salable, and then be prepared to act on the signs the market sends you. If you find lots of people visiting, but no one making an offer, there's something wrong and you may need to reduce your price. If no one is visiting, you almost certainly need to lower your price. Remember, a home's value is determined not by what you paid for it yesterday, but by what a willing buyer will pay for it today.

Turn no into yes—This is one instance where I'm not a big believer in lengthy appeals. Certainly engage in savvy negotiating, but don't spend lots of energy trying to squeeze every last dollar out of the deal. Sell for the best price you can get and move on with your life.

Part 5

Turning No into Yes When Facing Personal Problems*

*I truly believe that any rational no, whether in your business or your personal life, can be turned into a yes. However, I've only included three issues in this section of the book. That's because these are the three personal areas in which clients come to me for advice. While I know from firsthand experience that the same formula used to help you get a raise can also help you convince your spouse to take a beach vacation in the Bahamas rather than go sightseeing in Rome, the latter doesn't fall within my professional practice. I believe that in buying a book you're entitled to expert advice and so I've limited this section to those problems in which I'm clearly an expert. All that being said, if you have received a personal no that you'd like my help in turning around I'd be happy to help you out . . . as a friend. Just drop me a line care of HarperBusiness or send an E-mail message to me at mark4smp@aol.com.

Life Planning **36**

If you do not think about the future, you cannot have one.

John Galsworthy, Swan Song

I could write a book just about life planning. Actually I have. It's called *Die Broke*. Setting aside my own philosophies about the specific life planning events people come to me to ask for help with, and looking at those events solely in the context of problem solving, one thing stands out: most of my clients' worries stem from assumptions and expectations rather than facts.

It really is amazing how ingrained traditional ideas about life planning have become. I've had clients who pride themselves on their nonconformity never even think about whether the goals they're setting for their lives really make sense. Many simply assume they'll retire at age sixty-five, without even thinking about whether retirement makes sense for them at all, and if it does, whether age sixty-five is the right time. Clients who have striven to keep their offsprings' minds open to every possibility and opportunity automatically assume they should set aside enough tuition money for each of their children to go to private colleges. The struggling adult children of active and affluent seniors come to me with fears about taking care of their parents financially. And middle-aged parents who have already spent hundreds of thousands of dollars helping their children get through college and establish their adult lives bring me their woes about leaving sizable estates.

Most of my clients don't think about whether their goals make sense. They think these things are expected of them, and they're worried that they haven't yet been able to accomplish them. They assume every other parent has set aside enough money for four years of Bennington by the time a child is ten; that all their peers are saving and investing twenty-five percent of their income; that every other baby boomer already has $1 million in a retirement plan by the time they turn fifty; and that above and beyond retirement savings, everyone else is building up a huge estate to pass on to their children.

I don't want to spend dozens of pages setting out my arguments that retirement is a concept whose time has passed and shouldn't be a part of your planning, that all you can do for your parents and children is the best you can, and that it's better to spend your money on yourself and your family while you're alive than to pass it along in inheritance. If you're interested you can read my thoughts on these issues in *Die Broke*. What I think is important in this book is that I stress the foolishness of trying to do more than is possible, and the fallacy of comparing yourself to others.

At some point in your life you must accept the fact that you are not Superman or Wonder Woman. Success in life is measured, not by the size of your pile of chips, but by how well you played the hand you were dealt. You cannot control the economy or your generation's demographics. At some point you must come to terms with your own limitations. Unless you're lucky enough to become extremely wealthy, you simply will not be able to retire at sixty-five at the lifestyle you're used to, pay your child's entire college tuition bill, support aging parents until they die, and leave a huge estate. Set aside the question of whether or not you *should* do all these things. The simple truth is you probably won't be able to do all four of them, it's unlikely you'll be able to do three, and if you can do two it will only be after much personal sacrifice. The answer isn't to throw up your hands and give up; it's to do the best you can. The only person who expects any more than that is you.

Equally important is that you stop comparing yourself to others. There will always be individuals who are making more money than you . . . and there will always be people who are earning less. Some careers soar like rockets until they either settle into orbit or crash back down to earth. Others are like gliders, rising and falling gently, steering carefully to take advantage of thermals, staying aloft for as long as possible and then coming to a graceful and safe landing. Some businesses are sprinters, exploding out of the blocks and reaching top speed in a few strides. Others are marathoners, slowly building to a steady pace but then sticking to it for mile after mile. Life isn't about keeping score. It's not a means to an end. It's an end in itself.

I don't think I'll have enough to retire.

What's your problem?—If you have weighed the pros and cons and have decided you want to stop working at age sixty-five, this is your actual problem. If you haven't really thought about it, this is a presenting problem. Your actual problem is . . . that you haven't thought about it.

One problem at a time—Again, if you've given this some thought, then it's a single problem. However, if it's just a knee-jerk reaction, this is a cluster of problems, including lack of planning, feeling like a failure, and having insufficient savings, among others.

Focus on facts, not feelings—It's not enough to make retirement a conscious choice, you also need to be more specific in your planning. Is it that you don't have enough to retire at age sixty-five? What about by age seventy? Is it that you don't have enough to stop working totally? What if you work part-time when you turn sixty-five? This will remain an emotional issue until you frame it in specific terms. Only then will you be able to solve it.

Become an expert—The solution to this problem is becoming an expert on your own finances. When do you plan on retiring? How much money will you need to cover your expenses? How much will you be bringing in? Will you have an income from a pension? Will you have an income from a part-time job? How much will you have saved by that time? Will those savings generate an income for you? What do the numbers look like if you put off retirement for five years? What do they look like if you work part-time until age seventy-five? Should you invest your savings in a more aggressive manner? Should you be more conservative with your investments?

You can certainly do this planning on your own and do an excellent job. However I always encourage my clients to speak with a financial planner. I suggest hiring a fee-only planner to help develop a retirement program because he or she can provide expertise as well as an unbiased viewpoint. When it comes to buying specific investment products I strongly urge my clients to hire someone to help. It's enough to become an expert on your own needs and wants without also trying to become an expert on the constantly changing world of investments.

Create an environment of trust—Trust isn't an issue in this problem.

Turn no into yes—There is no appeal in this problem.

We're not saving enough money.

What's your problem?—This is almost always an actual problem, since almost no one in America is saving "enough" money.

One problem at a time—This is a single problem.

Focus on facts, not feelings—Despite it being a single actual problem, you'll have no luck solving it until you make it more specific. Until then it will remain an emotional issue. Let's agree that you're not saving enough money. However, for what are you saving? Are you not saving enough money to buy a home, to retire, to send your child to Harvard, to start a business? Unless you have a goal and a specific number in mind, you'll never be able to say you're saving enough.

Become an expert—Once again, the solution to this problem is to become an expert on your own finances. Sit down with your checkbook and credit card statements and figure out where all your money is going. Then, spend a month tracking all of your cash expenditures. Once you see where your money is going you can determine which expenses can be reduced, which can be trimmed, and which must stay the same. There's only one way to save money: spend less than you're earning. You can do that by maintaining your income while cutting your expenses, maintaining your expenses while increasing your income, or, for the best results, increasing your income and simultaneously cutting your expenses.

Interestingly enough, becoming aware of this problem is often the biggest step in solving it. Very few people will admit to not saving enough money, even though the problem is epidemic. Admitting you have the problem injects a certain degree of consciousness into your financial life. Sometimes, that—and fewer trips to the ATM—is all it takes.

If you find it difficult to restrain your spending, consider having your paycheck automatically deposited with a portion of it going immediately into some kind of savings plan. Perhaps if you don't have that money in your hands it will be easier for you not to spend it.

Create an environment of trust—Trust isn't an issue in this problem.

Turn no into yes—There is no appeal in this problem.

There's not enough for the kids' educations.

What's your problem?—If your child is at least ten years old then this is probably your actual problem. If your child isn't yet ten then it's apt to be a presenting problem, concealing problems of pride. Perhaps you're not saving enough in general but can't yet admit it. Maybe you're not making enough money at your job. Or it could be that you're comparing yourself to others whom you perceive to be more successful that you.

One problem at a time—When this is an actual problem, it's also a single problem. However, when this is a presenting problem it's actually covering up a cluster of different problems, most revolving around a sense that you're not doing as well financially as you think you should be doing, or as you think others are doing.

Focus on facts, not feelings—Expressed in this manner this is an irrational problem, whether it's your actual problem or not. What is enough? Enough to cover what the state expects parents to contribute to tuition at State U? Or enough to pay full tuition at Harvard? You need to come up with a number, or at least an estimate. Unless you have a finite target you'll never feel that you've put aside enough.

Become an expert—In order to come up with that target number you need to become an expert on college tuition, the means of paying it, and your own personal finances. Estimate what four years of room, board, and tuition will cost at a state or private school when your child is college age. You can find charts projecting these costs in any good book about paying for college.

With that cost estimate in hand you can then investigate the various subsidized and private loan, aid, and scholarship programs available. While the offerings will probably change by the time your child is ready for college, you can at least get a sense of what will be available for someone in your income bracket.

During your research you'll eventually come across the expected contributions of parents. This is an amount used in tabulating aid and loan packages. Every subsidized loan will automatically assume that you will be providing your child with that amount. If you aren't, you or your child will need to borrow that amount in a private loan. I tell my clients that their goal should be to provide their child with the amount of this expected contribution. If you do your best and fall short, the difference can be made up in loans. If you meet the goal, great. If you exceed it, that's even better. However, all you can do is your best.

Create an environment of trust—Trust isn't an issue in this problem.

Turn no into yes—There is no appeal in this problem.

What if I have to support my parents?

What's your problem?—This is an actual problem if your parents are either on shaky financial grounds or in poor health. If your parents are healthy and affluent it's probably a presenting problem, masking fears of increased responsibility, advancing age, and looming mortality.

One problem at a time—This is a single problem.

Focus on facts, not feelings—This is also a rational problem, since all too many older people do eventually need some kind of financial assistance.

Become an expert—As with all other life planning problems, the solution to the elder care issue is to become an expert in the field. Learn all you can about Medicare, Medicaid, nursing homes, home health care, and long-term care insurance. However, rather than focusing on your own finances as well, in this case you must become an expert on your parents' finances. How much of an income do they have? How secure is it? What are their assets? Are they liquid or frozen? What type of health insurance do they have? What will it cover and won't it cover?

In addition to becoming an expert on elder care issues and your parents' finances, you may need to help your parents hire other experts to provide the knowledge you lack. These might include an elder care attorney to help set up a Medicaid trust, a caregiver consultant to help arrange home-based health care, and a financial planner with experience working with senior citizens.

Create an environment of trust—In order to learn the details of your parents' finances and to help them hire professionals, you'll need to work on establishing trust. Obviously, a parent usually trusts their child. But when it comes to money there's often reticence.

Perhaps the parent is afraid of revealing information to a child's spouse. Or maybe the parent feels the child is out to take control of the finances. The secret to establishing financial trust with your parent is to paint every one of your questions and actions as being designed to help them. Stress that you're doing these things for their good, not yours. Bring other siblings into the picture if it will help. Have your parents select their own legal representative if that will make them feel more comfortable. Do whatever you can to make them understand that your goal is their comfort, not your own.

Turn no into yes—There is no appeal in this problem.

I'll have nothing to leave to my family.

What's your problem?—If you have a child who will in all likelihood not be able to take care of himself or herself as an adult, or you have unfulfilled financial obligations—say college tuition—to any of your children, then this is an actual problem. Otherwise this is a presenting problem, covering a poor self-image, fears of not measuring up to others, and worries of how the world will perceive you after you're gone.

One problem at a time—If this is your actual problem then it's a single problem. If this is a presenting problem it's a cluster of issues surrounding your misconceptions about inheritance and estates.

Focus on facts, not feelings—In order to look at this issue rationally you need to focus on whether or not there really is a need for you to provide for your family after your death. If there is, try to determine the extent of that need. For instance, if you need to provide for a young child's college education, you can estimate what that will cost. Or, if you need to provide a long-term income for a special needs child you can speak with a financial planner to figure out how large that income should be.

By looking at your postdeath obligations you narrow the issue to a finite, and solvable problem, rather than an open-ended, emotional problem of "providing" for your loved ones. Your value as a human being is determined not by the size of your estate but by the size of your heart. Provide for your family while you're alive and leave your children a legacy of love.

Become an expert—Once you've determined the size of your post-death obligations you need to become an expert on the financial tools that can help you meet those obligations: insurance.

A guaranteed renewable, straight term life insurance policy is, in my opinion, the best way to take care of most finite postdeath financial obligations. If you find out your child's college education will, when the time comes, cost you and your spouse $150,000 in parental contribution, get yourself a term life policy for that amount. If you live long enough to fulfill the obligation, then you can cancel the policy.

I believe the best way to take care of a child who may not be able to take care of himself or herself is to obtain what's called "second to die" insurance. This is a life insurance policy taken out on two lives, say you and your spouse, which only pays off after the second person dies. Because these policies cover two lives rather than one they're much cheaper than traditional policies. The concept is you assume that as long as one of the two parents are alive the child will be okay. The danger comes when both parents are dead and there's no one left to care for the needy child.

Create an environment of trust—Trust isn't an issue in this problem.

Turn no into yes—There is no appeal in this problem.

Prenuptials

37

There is no disparity in marriage like unsuitability of mind and purpose.

Charles Dickens, David Copperfield

I believe prenuptial agreements are justified in two situations: when one or both spouses are coming to the relationship with children not of this union; and when one or both spouses have important assets that are shared with other members of their family, such as a business.

In the first case, it's important that the children, rather than the new spouse, receive the assets their parent or parents grew for them. Let's say a fifty-three-year-old widow with two teenage children was planning on marrying a sixty-five-year-old widower with two grown children. It's important that the two teenagers inherit all the assets from their parents' union if their mother dies. Without a prenuptial agreement those assets would be divided with their stepfather. When he died, those assets would then also need to be split, with his children. The most common way these prenuptial agreements are structured is that the assets each individual brings to the marriage are designated for their own children, while the assets accumulated after the marriage go to the surviving spouse.

In the case of a family business, it's important the business remain in the hands of the owners rather than be passed on to a surviving spouse. For example, let's go back to that same fifty-three-year-old widow marrying the sixty-five-year-old widower. Say the widower and his three brothers have been running a furniture store, originally owned by their father. Were the widower to die, his wife, rather than his brothers or children, would be entitled to his one-fourth share of the business. The way these situations are often resolved is that in exchange for giving up any claim to the business, the company buys a life insurance policy on the owner's life that names the spouse as beneficiary. This could be handled in a shareholder's agreement, as well as a prenuptial agreement.

She/he thinks I don't trust her/him.

What's your problem?—This an actual problem.

One problem at a time—This is a single problem.

Focus on facts, not feelings—While the other person's perception that you lack trust is probably an emotional response, their rejection of your request is definitely a rational problem for you, since your goal of protecting your children or family business is entirely pragmatic.

Become an expert—Interestingly enough, this is a situation where you need to separate yourself from the expertise. It's essential that you make it clear to your future spouse that both of you will be represented by your own attorneys, and that the lawyers are the ones who should hammer out the details. As soon as you get involved in the specifics of the agreement the problem moves from a general effort to protect your family to a specific effort to get the better of the deal. The only people who should be expert in prenuptial agreements are lawyers.

Create an environment of trust—Obviously, the way to cure a lack of trust is to create trust. Start by making it clear in all you say and do that the marriage is not contingent on the signing of the prenuptial. Besides saying that, over and over, make sure you don't bring the issue up until after the two of you have agreed to marry. Explain that this actually has nothing to do with you and your future spouse; it has to do with your children or your family. This is a way to make them comfortable with the marriage, not you. By making sure that their financial interests are protected it gives them the chance to set those understandable fears aside and to embrace your union. The prenuptial is a way of taking care of obligations you've brought to this relationship; it's a tool so you can devote yourself to the future rather than worrying about the past.

Turn no into yes—There are two likely reasons for a rejection of a prenuptial request: that it's not fair, or that you shouldn't enter a relationship without full trust.

If fairness is cited, simply explain that with you both having your own attorney, fairness is guaranteed. That is an issue for the two lawyers to resolve, not for the two clients. Stress that, in fact, fairness is actually the goal of everyone—you, the lawyers, your children, and your business partners.

If a lack of trust is cited ("Don't you trust me to take care of your children?"), repeat again that it's not about your trust, but about the security of those who are depending on you. Stress that you obviously have complete and total trust in your future spouse. But say that your children or business partners wouldn't be human if they didn't have some fears about how they will be affected by a change in your marital status. The prenuptial is simply a way to overcome their fears, and it has nothing to do with you, your future spouse, or trust.

Divorcing

38

Marriage is a wonderful invention; but, then again, so is a bicycle repair kit.

Billy Connolly

Divorce is by its very nature an unpleasant experience. Nothing anyone can say or do will change that fact. However, there is one thing that you can do to make it less problematic and less costly: try to resolve the situation through mediation.

A mediator is a trained professional—sometimes, but not always, an attorney—who is hired by both parties in an effort to reach an agreement that is mutually acceptable. The mediator isn't an advocate for either side. Her interest is in getting the two of you to reach an agreement. If you and your soon to be ex-spouse both hire attorneys, the situation is dramatically different. An attorney is an advocate for one side. He is interested in getting the most he can for his client. In effect, an attorney is looking to win, and as a result, force the other side to lose, while a mediator is looking for both sides to win. Because there's only one professional involved in mediation, the costs are lower and the process is speedier.

I'm going to get robbed.

What's your problem?—This is a presenting problem. Your actual problem is that you're viewing the divorce as a win/lose situation.

One problem at a time—This is a single problem.

Focus on facts, not feelings—If you are in a traditional divorce proceeding in which both sides have lawyers, this is a rational fear. In those kinds of adversarial situations one party almost always ends up feeling like they've lost. Interestingly, the other party doesn't feel like a winner, they just feel satisfied, like they've gotten justice. If you're working with a mediator this is an irrational fear. The mediator's job is to make sure that neither party feels like they've been robbed.

Become an expert—This is one area where all the expertise should come from the hired professional.

Create an environment of trust—Ironically, trust is the most important factor in dissolving a marriage amicably. But due to the emotional nature of the situation neither party can hope to recreate trust in the other. The solution is to turn to a third party, the mediator, in whom both parties can place their trust.

Turn no into yes—There is no appeal to this problem.

What if I don't get custody?

What's your problem?—This is an actual problem.

One problem at a time—This is a single problem.

Focus on facts, not feelings—This is usually a rational problem.

Become an expert—This is a situation where the outcome is almost preordained. In most states, mothers who want to retain physical custody of children almost always will. The courts will bend over backward to keep children with their mother. For a father to get sole physical custody he will almost certainly need to demonstrate that the mother is clearly an unfit parent.

Legal custody is a separate issue. It's quite common for a father who has no physical custody to retain joint legal custody, so he retains a voice in major decisions in the child's life.

The parent who doesn't have physical custody is given visitation rights instead. A parent with visitation rights can often prevent a spouse with physical custody from moving to an area that would make visits more difficult. In fact, some courts forbid the parent with custody from leaving the general geographic area.

Create an environment of trust—If it comes down to a court battle, your attorney will help you do everything you can to demonstrate to the judge that you should be entrusted with the custody of your child. Unfortunately, your attorney will also need to do everything he can to demonstrate to the judge that your ex-spouse cannot be trusted. It won't be pretty.

Turn no into yes—Your attorney will be able to explain the best avenues for appeal if the decision goes against you.

I'm afraid I can't afford that much child support (or) I'm worried that won't be enough child support.

What's your problem?—These are all actual problems.

One problem at a time—They are also all single problems.

Focus on facts, not feelings—And they are all rational problems.

Become an expert—Once you learn about the divorce process you'll realize that while these are understandable fears, there's a system in place to make them irrelevant. Child support is a legal obligation, whether taken on voluntarily or imposed. The amount is generally a percentage of income, set either by statute, a judge's decision, or a binding agreement.* If someone stops paying child support they are breaking the law, just as if they suddenly stopped paying their taxes.

Create an environment of trust—This is one situation where both parties would do well to place their trust in an ironclad legal agreement rather than each other.

Turn no into yes—There is no appeal in this problem.

---

*By examining all the judges' decisions in a jurisdiction, you can come up with a rule of thumb. The binding agreements would be either prenuptial or separation.

Index